# MEMOIRS OF
# CAPTAIN J.M. BAILEY

Edited by James Troy Massey

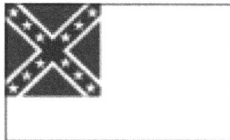

The Stainless Banner Publishing Company

www.thestainlessbanner.com

*Lovingly dedicated to the grandchildren: Clyde and Claude and John and Claude Moore Bailey, with the earnest hope that each and all of you may so live that when the summons comes that will call you hence, that you may go, as I hope to go, "Like one who draws around him the draperies of his couch and lies down to pleasant dreams."*

J.M. Bailey

*This book is dedicated to my grandson, Wyatt Troy Branch, who I hope will carry on the family torch of interest in history and particularly his Confederate past. And to my daughter, Whitney Massey Branch; my parents, Sam and Jo Ann Massey; and my wife, Beverly.*

J. Troy Massey

# PREFACE

I would like to extend many thanks to the people who have encouraged me to continue this project. First, I would like to thank James J. Johnston, who first made me aware of Captain Bailey's manuscript. Mr. Johnson is one of the foremost historians of the Arkansas-Missouri Ozarks history during the War Between the States. Thanks to Janice Ashworth, who completed some of the manuscript in the beginning. Many thanks to Diane Robb for typing this document and making the various text changes. She did the bulk of this work, or the manuscript would have been delayed. There was encouragement from Gene Waters and Dale Garner to keep working on this project.

My wife, Beverly and daughter, Whitney, are ever present and have given me time to continue my efforts to have this work published. They were there with encouragement and have never faltered. My parents, Samuel and Jo Ann Massey, told me to stay on track and keep working on this project for historical preservation. My brothers, Sam J., Jeffery and David Massey, who gave me that nudge to pick up the project again and finish the final chapter.

Thanks to Ronnie McDaniel for sharing Captain Bailey's post-war photo and military records. Ronnie married into the Bailey family and is interested in this subject. Also thanks for new found photos of the Baileys from their descendants, Steve Bailey, Ilse Bailey and Akil Grant in Texas and California. Toinette Madison of the Boone County Heritage Museum assisted in obtaining Captain Bailey's post war genealogical information and photos. Cassy Gray is to be commended for her publishing abilities. She encouraged me to have this book republished through her company, The Stainless Banner Publishing Company. Many thanks, Cassy!

Last, but not least, thanks to my Sons of Confederate Veteran's Camp – General Jo Shelby Camp No. 1414 and my Captain James Tyrie Wright Chapter Number 6, Military Order of the Stars and Bars of Harrison. The members were always interested in Captain Bailey's saga.

*The Guns of Port Hudson* relays Dr. A. M. Trackwick's account of Lieutenant Bailey. Trackwick, of Nashville, served as a young officer in the 16th Arkansas Infantry Regiment and commented, "I can still see in memory Lieutenant Bailey hunting for Lieutenant Spain with tears in his eyes."

At this writing, in 2013, I have completed other books, *Confederates Buried in Baxter, Boone, Carroll, Newton and Searcy Counties, Arkansas* and *Colonel John M. Harrell, A Brief Biography and Roster of Harrell's Arkansas Cavalry.* I also have a joint venture with my good friend, Rick Norton, of Springfield, Missouri, with a book entitled, *Hard Trials and Tribulations Of An Old Confederate Soldier by Captain George Maddox.*

I hope the reader enjoys this book, and it will provide a better understanding of the Southern perspective of our forefathers in the Ozark Mountains during the late War for Southern Independence.

James Troy Massey

CAPTAIN J.M. BAILEY

The writer of this sketch was born, according to records kept in my father's old family bible, January 28, 1841, in a pine log cabin on the waters of Ocoee River, in Polk County, Tennessee. My father, John Bailey, was born in Buncombe County, North Carolina, in 1794. My grandfather, William Bailey, was born in Virginia about the year 1764. The exact dates are not remembered. The old family bible, with its records of births, deaths, etc., was destroyed by Federal soldiers during the war. My great grandfather, William Bailey, came to Virginia from England sometime prior to the birth of grandfather.

Grandfather had no recollection of his parents, his mother dying in his infancy, and his father starting on a return voyage to England never again heard from by friends in Virginia. This is the story told grandfather by those who raised him.

When a few years old, grandfather was carried to North Carolina where he grew to manhood, serving during the latter part of the Revolutionary War with the patriot army. After the close of the war, he married a Miss Nancy Corn, of whose ancestors I know nothing, and settled in Buncombe County where he raised a family of seven children: two boys and five girls.

In the year 1818, with his family, he left the Old North State and moved over land by wagons drawn by ox teams to Missouri. Before reaching his destination in Missouri, he met a number of old friends and acquaintances returning from that territory, with fearful stories of sickness, death and hardships, who persuaded him to about face and seek a home nearer the bounds of civilization.

Having previously heard flattering reports of a section of country in East Tennessee, known as the Hiwassee Purchase,[*] he turned his course in that direction, arriving there in the winter of 1818-1819. He made a settlement on the Hiwassee River not far from the present town of Benton, the new county seat of Polk County. This was the home of the Cherokee Indians, and many of them still lived in the country around. To my father they gave the name "Bread."

Owing to the exposure and hardships incident to the early settlement, a malignant fever broke out in the family, from which two of my aunts died. My grandfather's family now consisted of five children, named as follows in the order of birth: Nancy, John, Lewis, Adelia, and Milita. Grandfather and grandmother spent the remainder of their days in Polk

---

*Spelling and punctuation have been modernized.

County, living several years before grandfather's death in a house built by my father near my boyhood home.

Many of my childhood hours were spent in their home listening with rapt attention to their tales of early days. Grandfather had been a great hunter, as were most of the early settlers in the West, and was very fond of telling hunting stories that were very interesting to me. He was still fond of his old flintlock rifle that he kept on a rack just over the door. Notwithstanding his great age, then over 80 years, he could see well enough to kill squirrels, and as they were then plentiful, he often took me with him on his short hunts.

My recollections of grandfather are very distinct. He was tall and slender, with regular features and very straight for a man of his age. His hair was white. I never saw him with a beard over a few days old. Very few men wore beards at that time. My recollections of grandmother are not so clear.

Grandfather died in 1848 after a brief illness, in the 84th year of his age. His dying was my first realization of the meaning of death, and many years passed before the picture of his face in death passed from my memory. Grandmother died about the year 1856.

My father was married to my mother, Miss Bershaba Cunningham, daughter of Joseph Cunningham of Monroe County, Tennessee, about 1823, and settled near my grandfather's old home on the Hiwassee River. Some years later, he bought from the government 160 acres of land south of the Ocoee River, where I was born, and where he resided till the fall of 1853.

Six children were born to my parents, named in the order of their birth as follows: Malinda Jane, April 17, 1825; William Wilson, May 4, 1827; John Meriman, July 6, 1829; Caloway

Shields, ____(January 4), 1832; Lewis Washington, August 30, 1838, and the writer as above written.

Of my mother's people, I knew but little. Her mother died when she was quite young. My Grandfather Cunningham, I saw only once when I was about seven years old. My recollections of him are not very distinct, though I remember that he, like my Grandfather Bailey, was tall and slender. He died at his home in Monroe County, Tennessee, about the year 1858.

My father's education was limited to a knowledge of reading, writing and enough of mathematics for ordinary business transactions. His business was that of a farmer and stock raiser in a small way.

My recollections of the old home where I was born are that it was very poor piney woods land, as were most of the uplands of East Tennessee. Only by untiring industry and strict economy was it possible for a man to support with any degree of comfort a family.

Educational advantages for the children of an ordinary farmer were limited to a three months course in the public or subscription schools, which usually began with the laying by of crops in July or August. I attended with more or less irregularity four terms of such schools, receiving my first knowledge of the "three R's," with a slight smattering of grammar and geography. I also received a liberal share of corporal punishment, which was administered in those days without stint.

In the fall of 1852, my two oldest brothers, William and Meriman, left the old home for the "far West," settling in Carroll County, Arkansas. Their leaving home was the first separation of members of our family and was very trying on all of us, but especially so to my mother, who grieved much over the absences of her children.

In the fall of 1853, my father sold the farm and most of the household goods, loading the balance with other necessary equipment in two wagons, one drawn by two yoke of oxen and the other by a pair of horses, and started on the 800 mile journey to the home of my brothers. After an uneventful trip of seven weeks, we arrived safely, much to the joy of all of us, as there was a strong bond of affection existing among the members of the family and this had been our first separation.

★ ★ ★

In the Crooked Creek Valley a few miles above the present town of Harrison, my father bought 400 or 500 acres of land and settled down to spend the remainder of his life in the quiet pursuit of farming and stock raising.

The years passed on; one by one the older brothers married and were living within a few miles of my father's homestead. Children came to gladden their homes and to brighten the declining years of the grandparents, who were now nearing the three score mile post on life's journey. Peace, plenty and quiet for the remainder of their lives seemed assured.

But soon the ominous mutterings of the Great War that swept the country from '61 to '65 were heard, gathering force and volume as it came. My father, as were most of the people in that section of the country, was devotedly attached to the Union and had very pronounced views on the question of slavery; believing it was wrong, viewed from any standpoint.

But when the struggle came, he was heart and soul for the country of his birth.

With tear dimmed eyes and aching hearts, my parents bid good-bye to their five sons, who volunteered for service in the Confederate Army, little hoping for the safe return of all of them. While left practically alone, so far as male help was concerned, they managed to live with tolerable comfort for the first 12 months of the war. My sister and one brother's wife and child were living with them. Being near the border, the country was soon overrun by first one and then the other of the contending forces; until war, with all of its horrible cruelties, was being enacted all around the old homestead.

In the early part of the war, nearly all the able bodied men in that part of the country volunteered for service in the Confederate Army. But later on, when the enemy occupied the country in force and the result of the war seemed at least doubtful, many deserted their colors and joined the Union Army. To these men most of the cruelties and wanton destruction of property was due.

By the latter part of '63, nearly all the horses, cattle, sheep and hogs belonging to my father had either been killed or driven off, and the family was left practically destitute of the means of making the barest living. To add to all this, the old home was wantonly set on fire by men wearing the uniform of Federal soldiers and reduced to ashes, with nearly every item of household goods.

My mother and sisters endeavored to save some of the more cherished articles of household goods, but a brutal soldiery threw most of it back into the flames. These were regular soldiers, officered by men bearing commissions as such from the Government at Washington. I regret now that I cannot call to mind the particular command, which I once knew. They claimed to be acting under orders of superior officers.

Thrown out of doors in dead of winter, they found shelter in the home of one of my brothers. No act of vandalism had even been charged against any member of my father's family as a justification for this outrage. That my father was a Southern man and his sons were in the Confederate Army was the only cause. My father's family spent the remainder of the winter and the following spring at my brother's home undergoing many hardships and privations.

In the summer following, at the friendly request of a Union family, who lived near my father's old home, they occupied their home, as they were going north. A short stay in this Union man's house, and it shared the same fate – burned to the ground by Federal soldiers.

Later on, they fitted up an old log cabin on the old homestead that had been used for years as a corn crib and other like purposes and lived in it till the spring of 1865, when it shared a similar fate at the hands of men wearing the blue. They then fitted up as best they could an old log stable of two stalls, about 12'-0" x 14'-0" in size each, with the bare earth for flooring and a leaky roof that admitted about as much water as it shed off.

In this stable they were living when peace, "white winged" and welcome came in the summer of 1865. In this old log stable, they lived to see the return of their five sons, four of whom bore scars won in battle for home and country. That they suffered extreme hardships for want of food, clothing and shelter is well known to all those who lived on or near the border between the contending forces, but all their physical suffering was nothing compared to the mental anguish they suffered during the four years of bloody strife.

During the last months of the war, they often went for days without meat or bread of any kind, not even salt to season the little food they had. For days they lived upon salads, made of young shoots of polk stalks, tongue grass and other edible vegetation, without salt, simply boiled. This slight sketch of the suffering of my father's family was the fate of other Southern families, varied only by degrees of more or less severity. Such luxuries as sugar, coffee, tea and rice were unknown among the people in North Arkansas during the last three years of the war, except in very rare cases.

★ ★ ★

To illustrate something of the cruelties and barbarities of war, I will write one incident. During the winter of 1862-63, when that part of the country was overrun by Federal troops, a regiment of cavalry came by my father's home, having as prisoners three young men, neighbor boys, about 18 to 20 years of age, whom they had just captured. After a short stop at the house, they passed on, taking the prisoners with them.

Shortly after, the family heard a volley of small arms in the direction they had taken. Suspecting the worst, my sisters followed their trail. About one mile away, they found the lifeless bodies of William Easter and Ben Womack lying by the road side. After looking around for some time for the other young man, Calvin Rutledge, they heard groans from a distance in the thick woods where they found him suffering from no less than seven separate bullet wounds. They cared for him as best they could, summoned help as quickly as possible and carried him some miles away to a secluded place in the woods where he was nursed back to health, apparently none the worse for his many wounds.

Incidents of this character were frequent occurrence, the victims often being old men and noncombatants, some of who were past three score years and ten. While much of the cruelty was due to deserters from the Confederate Army, the volunteer forces from the North were guilty of many inexcusable acts of brutality, such as house burnings and killing prisoners. The foreign born soldiers in the Union Army, Germans especially, were brutal and cruel in their treatment of the people. There were some notable exceptions, where officers and men treated the people with kindness.

★ ★ ★

My parents lived to see not only the return of their lives comparative comfort, honored and respected by a large circle of friends. My father was a man of robust constitution, 5'-10" and weighed about 175 pounds. He died after a brief illness, at the home of his only daughter, Mrs. M.J. Rosson, at Bellefonte, Arkansas, October 1, 1876, and was buried at White Church not far from his old home on Crooked Creek.

My mother in appearance was a frail bit of humanity, weighing usually less then 100 pounds, but endowed with wonderful powers of endurance. She retained her mental and physical vigor to a remarkable degree. She frequently rode horseback several miles without great weariness, after she had attained the age of 90 years. She died after a few days illness at the home of my sister, Mrs. Rosson, on the 27th day of September, 1889, and was buried by the side of him who had shared her joys and sorrows for over 50 years.

Before proceeding further with this sketch, I would pay a brief tribute to the memory of my sister, to whose gentle admonitions and kindly advice I am at least, partly indebted for whatever worth I may have attained. But it is of her loyal, untiring devotion to our parents that I care most to write. Always kind, gentle and patient, she ministered to their every want; a companion in health and in sickness; a nurse. With the same unselfish devotion and tender care she nursed her husband, Captain John Rosson (Harrell's Arkansas Cavalry Battalion) through months of painful suffering till death came to his relief. On the 11th day of February, 1903, after a long and painful illness, she died at her home in Harrison, Arkansas and was laid to rest by the side of her husband in the Harrison Cemetery, honored and loved by all who knew her.

★★★

After my father settled in North Arkansas in 1853, I worked on the farm. In the fall of 1854, I attended a private school for two months. This, with the schooling already mentioned, constituted the sum total of my time spent in school. I had a fondness for books, however, and spent a good part of my spare time in reading such books as we were fortunate enough to own, which was limited to a very few volumes. History, especially of wars, and personal adventures were the books that interested me most. Pictures of battle scenes had a fascination for me that enthralled my boyish fancy.

I cared less for society than most young people, and, as well as I now remember, I never attended a social gathering of young folks up to the time I was 20 years of age. I was content to labor on the farm, visit and receive visits from a few neighboring boys of about my age and reading such books as I was able to get.

Owing to my fondness for books, coupled with a good deal of persistence on my part, my father had agreed that I might enter Cane Hill College in Washington County in the fall of 1861; but the breaking out of the war brought an end to my hopes of an education.

When President Lincoln issued the call for 75,000 men to coerce the South, the war spirit in Northern Arkansas, where I lived, was thoroughly aroused. Meetings were held in every village and neighborhood, and steps taken looking to the organization of companies for service in defense of the South should the country be invaded by Northern troops. Many yet hoped for a peaceful solution of the pending trouble, but the rapid march of events soon dispelled all their hopes.

Under a call for Arkansas State troops, I joined the first company that was organized in my part of the country. It was made up almost entirely of farmers ranging in age from 16 to 40 years. All were ignorant of war and military training. Not one of the numbers had ever seen service anything more than the light training they had had in the militia service, which usually amounted to a few hours drill once or twice a year. But what they lacked in training, they made up in patriotic devotion to their country, which, after all, is the best foundation on which to build the highest types of soldiery.

The first Confederate flag made in that part of the country was made at my father's house by my sister and Miss J.B. Wright and later presented to the company to which I belonged by Miss Wright, in a patriotic address, eloquently delivered. In her honor, the company was named the "Joe Wright Guards."[1]

A few days after the organization of the company, orders came to report without delay to Camp Walker in Washington County, Arkansas, about 90 miles distant. Every member of the company reported present when the roll was called. Many left the plow in midfield. I well remember that I was laying by corn; giving it the last plowing, when the summons came, and left unplowed a number of rows. What memories come trooping up as I recall the thrilling events of that memorable time: The old home of my boyhood, blotted out by the "red torch of war," but from my memory, never. The friends of *Auld Lang Syne*. The call to arms. The hurried gathering of those who wore the gray. The music of fife and drum, how it thrilled us! The tender good-byes that were said. The march away from home to the music of that dear old tune, *The Girl I Left Behind Me*, and who of us was not leaving behind some one dearer than all other? I confess that there was a slender, dark-eyed, brown haired girl who had won my deepest love, and who I believed felt more than a passing interest in me.

---

[1]The officers of the "Joe Wright Guards" were John Smith, captain; my brother, W.W. Bailey, first lieutenant; Jeff Greenlee, second lieutenant; Joe Owens, third lieutenant; Jones Johnson, orderly sergeant. Captain Smith resigned after a brief service, and Sergeant Johnson was elected and remained in command till the company mustered out of service later on. J.M.B.

A march of five days and we were at Camp Walker, where were assembled 3,000 or 4,000 men under General Ben McCulloch. What a change from the quiet of the peaceful country home to the noise and stir of a military camp! The white tents, the beat of drums, the bugle call, the tramp of armed men, the bright gleam of bayonets, and, high above all, proudly floating in the breeze, the flag of the new born nation to which we had pledged our fealty.

A few days in camp with earnest, awkward attempts at drill. A few days later, borne on the summer breeze, came the boom, boom of artillery, far to the north, but each shot sounding clear and distinct, which told us that the enemy was not far away and that the war was a reality. How the boom of those guns thrilled me and made strong the desire to be an active participant in a battle. A feeling, I think, that was shared almost universally by all the men in camp. In fact, I think, most of us feared that it would not be our good fortunes to be engaged in battle.

★ ★ ★

About August 1st, we took up the line of march towards Springfield, Missouri, then occupied by Federal troops under General (Nathaniel) Lyon. On the way we were joined by the Missouri troops under General (Sterling) Price. A few days march over hot dusty roads, a few skirmishes in front, in which the rattle of small arms was heard for the first time. A few wounded men being conveyed back to the rear. A few new made graves by the road side gave us our first impressions of what war was like.

The evening of the 7th day of August, we camped on Wilson Creek, a beautiful clear running stream of water – ten miles distant from Springfield. Late on the evening of the 9th, we received orders to be in readiness to march at a moment's notice, evidently with the intention of attacking the enemy at Springfield the next morning. Quietly we waited; hours passed and still no order to march. Midnight came and the men were quietly sleeping, dreaming perhaps of home and loved ones. The early dawn of August the 10th found us still waiting. There was life once more in camp. Some were making fires preparatory to cooking their morning meal; some of the earlier risers were eating their breakfast.

Looking over the valley to the west, across the creek, where the public road that led to Springfield passed through our camps, I saw a lone horseman riding at breakneck speed in the direction of headquarters, leaving behind him a long trail of dust. A moment later, a hatless courier rode with the speed of the wind through our camp. Boom! And a shell went shrieking through the tree tops overhead followed by others in rapid succession.

"Fall into line!" was heard on every side. With the bearing and confidence of veterans of many battle, these men, fresh from the plow handles, took their places in line and marched away to the various positions assigned them. The Joe Wright Guards had been assigned to the 4th Arkansas Infantry, commanded by Colonel Dave Walker. This regiment was ordered to support Reid's Arkansas Battery, which was quickly placed in position on a high point east of the creek, overlooking the valley to the west and giving an excellent view of the greater part of the battleground. Reid's guns, some 50 yards away, went into action at once. A few shells from the enemy's guns dropped near us, but no assault was made on our position.

In other parts of the field, the firing of artillery and small arms was terrific. Yells of the contending forces came over the smoke laden air to die away later to be renewed, whether by friend or foe, we could not tell. Hours passed and still the battle raged. Men standing in line in that hot August sun grew thirsty and called for water. A detail was ordered with canteens to bring water from a spring – some 200 or 300 hundred yards distant. I was one of that detail.

While filling the canteens, a wagon was drawn up near the spring. Passing by the hind end of the wagon, which was open, I beheld the ghastly forms of a number of dead Confederate soldiers. Looking at the upturned faces of these men from which the life blood had ebbed away, stained as they were with blood and dust – the grime of battle – what a picture for the inexperienced eyes of a boy fresh from the peace and quiet of the old country home!

A memory of the old farm flitted across my mind: the unplowed corn rows, the jingle of cow bells, the song of birds. A momentary heart longing for its peaceful scenes. The picture that had so impressed me vanished when I returned to the thirsty, eager, confident comrades, standing in line, expecting every moment to take a hand in the battle that was yet raging with unabated fury.

Gradually the enemy was driven back and shouts of triumph told us that they were in full retreat and that the victory was ours. By noon, the echoes of the last gun had died away among the surrounding hills.

Obtaining permission from my captain, with a young friend who later gave his life to the Southland, we started out to view the battleground. Passing through a cornfield to the north, we saw our first Federal dead lying among the corn rows; hands and faces blackened by the heat of that August sun. Turning west across the creek, on what was afterwards called "Bloody Hill," on which the severest fighting took place, we found great numbers of Federal dead and wounded.

Some of the wounded, groaning and writhing in agony; others in silence, patiently bearing their suffering. One poor fellow, with both legs mangled, the death pallor on his face, muttered in half audible words, bitter curses about being "deserted." Holding my canteen to his lips, he drank deeply, looking the thanks his lips failed to speak. To other wounded we gave water till the contents of our canteens were exhausted.

Over the heads of some of the wounded, friends – and all were friends now – had stuck bushes to ward off the sun's hot rays. Here and there horses were dead or in the agonizing throes of death. Everywhere the grass was trampled down, bushes and small saplings were crushed and broken, where artillery had wheeled into position, advanced or hastily retreated. Here and there crimson stains blended with the green of the leaves and grass, or formed a darker hue as it mingled with the dust of the ground.

On this hill, General Lyon was killed. His horse, a fine gray, fell near the same spot. The horse's mane and tail had been closely clipped and carried away as souvenirs by the Confederates.

A hurried visit to the hastily improvised hospital of tents, where surgeons and their assistants were busy dressing wounds and amputating limbs, amid groans and shrieks that were simply appalling. Trenches were hastily dug where our Confederate dead were laid side by side, uncoffined, to "sleep their manhood away." Most of the Federal dead remained unburied till next day.

Late that evening, we moved camps some three or four miles up the creek, where we spent several days. When not on duty, I spent my spare time strolling over the battleground, till I became familiar with every hill and valley. One of the things that impressed me was the entire absence of bird life. Not even a vulture flapped its wings in the carrion scented air.

In the course of three or four days, all of the wounded had been removed to Springfield and the battleground was deserted. On the 6th day after the battle, a young friend, Lish Robertson, (possibly Private Lewis Robertson, Co. K, 16th Arkansas) and I strolled again, for the last time, over the field.

A white object in a thick cluster of post oak runners attracted our attention. On investigation, we found the lifeless form of a boy lying on a pallet of straw, his only covering a white sheet. He was apparently about sixteen years of age, light haired and slender, with features almost girlish in looks. On his lips, half parted, the lingering trace of a smile.

An ugly wound in the left side revealed the cause of death. With folded hands on his pallet of straw, we left him alone in his dreamless sleep. Who he was, whether he wore the blue or gray, we never knew.[2] With the new morning's sunrise, we were on the march and away.

---

[2] I have always supposed that the boy was among the last to die in the field hospital and that the detail left to bury the dead grew tired of their work and quietly laid the body in this secluded place and doubtless reported all

★ ★ ★

About the 20th of August, the Arkansas State Troops were disbanded. A few weeks later under a call from the Confederate States, another company was organized which I joined. J.H. Williams was elected captain. My brother, W. W. Bailey, 1st lieutenant; Israel Sigman (Co. D, 16th Arkansas) and E.M. Spain (Elbert M. Spain, Co. D, 16th Arkansas), 2nd and 3rd lieutenants.

On the discharge of the "Joe Wright Guards," their old flag was returned to Miss Wright and was by her again presented to the newly organized company, and by the captain, handed to me as company color bearer. Again the goodbyes were said, by many who never again clasped hands, and we took up the line of march to Fayetteville, Arkansas, where we were joined by other companies, ten in all, forming the 16th Arkansas Infantry, Colonel J.F. Hill, commanding. How proud I felt when our company flag was selected from half a score as the regimental colors, and prouder still when the Colonel named me as regimental color bearer, with the rank of sergeant. The regiment went into camps at Elm Springs in Washington County where we remained till about February 20, 1862. The winter was spent in drill and other duties incident to camp life.

---

bodies buried. I recall the feeling of envy with which I looked upon the men of the various commands who lost heavily in killed and wounded and felt humiliated over the fact that my own regiment fired not a shot nor shed one drop of blood. J.M.B.

★ ★ ★

About the 20th of February, we received orders to join other troops under General McCulloch who had spent the winter at points not far distant, and proceed toward Springfield, Missouri, and effect a junction with the troops under General Price, who were falling back from that place, hotly pressed by a superior force of Federals under Generals (Samuel) Curtis and (Franz) Sigel.

At Cross Hollows in Benton County, Arkansas, we met the forces under General Price, slowly retreating before the enemy. We marched all day and the night following, reaching Cross Hollows early in the morning, thoroughly tired and hungry. A rest of about two hours and the retreat was resumed.

Severe skirmishing between the enemy's advanced forces and our rear guard occurred during the day. Several times we formed line of battle marching and counter marching till by nightfall, when we went into camps, we felt thoroughly exhausted; having been on the tramp for about 36 hours, with no sleep and very little rest. A good night's sleep and we felt all right for the next day's march.

The Confederates continued the retreat to Boston Mountain, some 25 miles south of Fayetteville. The Federal forces established headquarters at Pea Ridge, Benton County. We remained in camp on Boston Mountain a few days, while all the available forces of the Confederates were being concentrated.

About this time, General (Earl) Van Dorn assumed command of the combined forces of Generals McCulloch and Price and, on the 3rd or 4th day of March, we took up the line of march towards the enemy at Pea Ridge. On the 6th of March, our advanced guard was in touch with the enemy. More or less skirmishing ensued during the day between the opposing forces.

The march was continued at intervals all of the following night. Halts were frequent but of short duration. We would lie down by the road side to be roused up in a few minutes. While we marched only a few miles during the night, yet we had no time for sleep.

On the morning of March 7th, the attack was made from the north, having passed to the west of the enemy's left flank. McCulloch commanded the right wing of the Confederates and General Price the left. After severe fighting for the greater part of two days, the Confederates withdrew from the field, leaving most of our dead and wounded.

The 16th Arkansas Infantry was under fire more or less during both days and lost quite a number in killed and wounded. General McCulloch was killed early in the engagement on the morning of the 7th, which in all probability, lost to us the battle as General (James) McIntosh, next in command, was killed about the same time and General (Louis) Hérbert was wounded, leaving the right wing without an officer higher in rank than a colonel. Colonels of regiments without orders, and, not knowing of the death of their commanders, acted on their own responsibility, which naturally led to more or less confusion and lack of concerted action.

Had McCulloch lived, doubtless a combined and vigorous assault would have been made on the enemy's position in a very short time as the troops were already in position for such a movement. Lines were formed facing the enemy only a short distance in our front. The men were eager for the fray and confident of victory.

As I have never seen any published account of General McCulloch's death, I will state what came under my observation. So far as I could see and know, my regiment formed the extreme right of the right wing of our infantry. After some skirmishing and a charge of mounted men to our right in which a Federal battery was captured, the infantry moved forward in line of battle, halting in some timber a hundred or more yards north of a field, lying east and west and apparently 300 or 400 hundred yards across from north to south. From this position, we could get glimpses of the army on the south side of the field who gave us a few rounds of grape and canister.

We had occupied this position only a few minutes when General McCulloch came riding along in front of our line passing from left to right. He spoke a few words in passing, but I am now unable to recall the words. When near the right of the regiment, he ordered one or two companies, two I think, forward as skirmishers and rode on along into some rather thick woods to our right. He was carrying, as was his custom, a short breech loading rifle and field glasses.

In a very short time after he passed out of sight, the regiment was ordered by the right flank to a position some 200 yards to our right, then forward right oblique through thick woods to the fence on the north side of the field to drive a line of Federal skirmishers from the fence across the field. Colonel Hill passing near ordered me to lower the flag as it showed above the bushes and was drawing fire from the enemy's artillery.

Feeling at liberty to leave my position, I passed along the line to the right where my brother W.W. Bailey was in command of my old company (Captain Williams having fallen out from exhaustion) to learn what loss, if any, they had sustained.

Before reaching my old company, a young man named Jones, some 40 steps to the right and rear, called to me saying: "Come here, here is General McCulloch." He was lying full length on his back with a bullet wound in his right breast. A bit of white cotton patching, such as was used at that time in the make up of cartridges for the Mississippi or old squirrel rifles was sticking in the hole made by the bullet in his coat. This showed conclusively that he had been killed by one of the Federal skirmishers from behind the fence, as some of their dead and wounded near the fence were armed with Mississippi rifles.

I reported to Lieutenant (B.T.) Pixlee, adjutant of the regiment, who was only a few steps away, who took off his overcoat and threw it over General McCulloch's body, covering his face with the cape saying: "We must not let the men know that General McCulloch is dead."

About this time Colonel (F.A.) Rector's regiment of Arkansas infantry (17th) passed by, going to our right. Some of the officers inquired who that was, pointing to the dead body. Lieutenant Pixlee answered, "Sergeant _____."

His horse, gun, fieldglasses and watch were gone. A detail of four men from my old company carried his body to the rear, which was later sent to Texas for burial. He had evidently started to the field to reconnoiter and was picked off by a sharpshooter not over 40 yards away. Whether he was killed from his horse or had dismounted we never knew.

Before forming lines of battle on the morning of March 7th, the men of my regiment deposited their blankets (each man carried one) in a heap by the roadside, leaving them in care of a guard. In withdrawing from the field that evening, we found the guard missing and that our blankets had been taken by other troops – Indians under General Pike.

Some hours after the death of General McCulloch, my regiment, and I think practically all of the right wing, was ordered to retire from that part of the field in which we had been engaged and take a position just in rear of the left wing, a short distance north of the old Elkhorn Tavern from which the Federals had been driven during the day.

That night we had for a bed the bare ground and the sky for a covering. For supper and breakfast we had a ration of flour only, which we made into dough with cold water and baked as best we could, without any kind of cooking vessels. The usual method was to roll the dough around a ramrod and hold it over the fire till done. Our sleep was disturbed that night by the rattle of ambulances and the groans of wounded men being conveyed to a hospital a short distance in our rear.

In the early dawn, we marched by the old tavern with the great elk horns, from which it took its name. All around were many evidences of desperate fighting the day previous. We were soon placed in position, forming a second line; the first about 100 yards in our front.

About sunrise the enemy's artillery opened a terrific fire on our lines which they kept up for several hours. The firing of small arms was irregular and severe at any time. About noon, if my recollection serves me right, orders came to fall back a short distance and then retire from the field. The order was a surprise to us as we supposed the battle would be renewed and had been expecting orders for a forward movement for hours. The retreat was severely criticized by many. So far as my personal observation went, the men were in good condition for fighting. At no time was there the slightest evidence of panic or lack of confidence. The withdrawal was leisurely and without confusion. There was no attempt at pursuit.

That night we camped about ten miles from the battleground at what was called Van Winkle's Mill. It had rained very hard during the evening and to keep off of the damp ground, I slept on a piece of plank.

There were a number of shoats weighing perhaps 40 or 50 pounds running around our camps. Some mounted men came riding by and one of them called out: "Hand me one of those shoats" when Sergeant Rush of my company stuck his bayonet through one of them and held it up to the cavalry man, who took it and rode on with the squealing pig under his arm.

The march south was resumed next morning. The day following we remained in camp. Under orders to report with his command at Corinth, Mississippi, General Van Dorn continued the march south across Boston Mountain via Clarksville on the Arkansas River. Then east to De Valls Bluff on the White River – a march of something over 200 miles.

At De Valls Bluff, we took passage on a river steamer going down the White River to the Mississippi, then up the Mississippi to Memphis where we took the cars to Corinth, arriving there a few days after the Battle of Shiloh or Pittsburg Landing. For several days we camped near Corinth and then occupied camps some miles south near a little town called Rienzi. After a stay of about ten days at this place, we

Memoirs of Captain J.M. Bailey

were ordered back to Corinth. During all of this time, the roar of artillery was heard daily to the north of Corinth and only a few miles away.

About this time, my regiment was presented with a new flag, designed as a battle flag. Folding up my old flag, I placed it in my bosom for safe keeping, where I carried it for over 12 months.

☆ ☆ ☆

About the last of April, my brother Lieutenant (W.W.) Bailey resigned on account of ill health. He had been in command of the company since the Battle of Elkhorn. Captain Williams was captured there and never rejoined the company. Lieutenant Sigman also resigned about this time. On the 8th of May, 1862, a reorganization of the command was ordered. Captain David Province (3rd Arkansas [State Troops] and 16th Arkansas) of Rivers' Battery was elected colonel. Lieutenant and acting Adjutant Pixlee, lieutenant colonel; (J.M.) Pittman, major; E.G. Mitchell was elected captain of Company D, my old company. John Brittain, lst lieutenant. The writer, 2nd lieutenant and E.M. Spain was re-elected 3rd lieutenant. Mark Buchannan (Private Co. G, 16th Arkansas) of Company C (G) succeeded me as color bearer of the regiment. A few weeks later, with vacancies occurring above me, I was promoted to the rank of 1st lieutenant, and Sergeant Rush was elected 2nd lieutenant.

The regiment was engaged in the fight at Farmington, in the early part of May, and later took an active part in the defense of Corinth, doing picket duty and engaging in a

25

number of skirmishes, in which quite a number of men were killed or wounded.

After the evacuation of Corinth, the Confederates went into camp at Okolona about 40 miles south of Corinth. The only sickness I had during the war was while stationed at this place. A stay of two weeks in a hospital at Enterprise, Mississippi, and I was again able for duty.

In the early part of September, there was evidence of a forward movement, which resulted a few days later in an attack on and capture of Iuka, Mississippi, situated a few miles east of Corinth.

We remained at Iuka three or four days when, on the evening of September 19th, the Federals under General (Ulysses S.) Grant made an attack upon our left flank. The fight, though of short duration, was hotly contested, with results in favor of the Confederates who held the battleground and captured a six gun battery.

At the beginning of the fight, the 16th Arkansas and four Missouri regiments, forming what was called the 1st Missouri Brigade under General (Lewis) Little, occupied a position about three miles west of Iuka and towards Corinth expecting an attack from that direction.

We were double quicked to the scene of action, going into line of battle about dusk and just before the firing ceased, occupying the battleground where the Federal battery was captured. General Little was killed just as we went into line.

The Federals had fallen back only a short distance as we could hear them plainly and were fired on several times during the night. Most of the dead and wounded of the enemy lay where they fell, some of them between the opposing lines. Their moans and calls for help and water were pitiful in the extreme. The cry of one poor fellow not far away was "John, oh, John." Quite a number of the wounded in less exposed parts of the field were carried back a short distance and laid in the yard of a farmhouse some 200 or 300 hundred yards to our rear.

Added to the groans of the wounded men was the rattling of chains and harness on wounded artillery horses, only a few yards away. The captured guns were only a few steps to our rear. Till midnight I was officer of the guard, which made it necessary for me to visit our pickets or guards, about 30 steps in our front to see that all was well. With the silent forms of the dead lying among the cluster of bushes as I passed from sentry to sentry, my feelings can be better imagined than described.

When relieved at midnight, I lay down with the men in line of battle but not to sleep. As the hours passed, the moans and calls grew less frequent. The last hours of the night grew comparatively quiet, save the struggling of the wounded horses in their harness.

We confidently expected a renewal of the fight with the coming of day, but to our surprise, just as day dawned, we withdrew, leaving the battleground and the captured guns in possession of the enemy. We returned to a point near our old camp at Okolona where we remained in camp a few days. Again we took up the line of march approaching Corinth from the west.

On the 3rd of October, after more or less skirmishing and some pretty severe fighting, the enemy withdrew to their main line of defense around Corinth. Our line of battle was formed that evening in easy range of their guns but hid from view by intervening skirts of timber.

With the break of day on the morning of the 4th, our artillery, from a ridge in our rear, opened fire on the town and its line of defenses. A few minutes later the enemy's guns replied with vigor. This artillery fire was kept up till about 9:00 a.m., when the order to move forward was given by General Gates, then in command of the brigade, in a voice that could have been easily heard a mile away.

Passing through a narrow belt of timber, we emerged into open ground in full view of the enemy's breastworks lining the crest of a ridge, some 300 yards in our front. The enemy's artillery opened a terrific fire on our line as soon as we showed in the open ground, but there was no wavering.

Steadily the men went forward to meet a death dealing fire from both artillery and infantry, but there was no halt till the crest of the hill was reached and the works captured with pieces of artillery. To our right, a more vigorous defense was made, and the assaulting line was compelled to retreat.

Looking to our right, I could see, through the smoke that nearly enveloped the crest of the hill, our broken line falling back. Soon the enemy's guns, along the defenses to our right from which our troops had been repulsed, were turned on us, raking our lines from one end to the other.

The order to retreat was given by Colonel (F.M.) Cockrell of Missouri, then a colonel of one of the Missouri regiments composing the 1st Missouri Brigade. Hastily, and with no regard to order, we retreated to the friendly shelter of the timber, leaving our dead and most of our wounded where they fell. I have often thought of the havoc a few companies of cavalry could have made had they been hurled on us at the right moment.

Our broken lines were reformed about 3/4ths of a mile from the scene of our repulse. Buchannan, our gallant color bearer, planted our color on the breastworks and escaped unhurt, but the color bearers of the other regiments of the brigade were either killed or wounded. Company D lost several men, in killed or wounded, among the latter was Lieutenant Rush, who died a few days later. Lieutenant Colonel Pixlee was severely wounded but was assisted from the field. Lieutenant (James H.) Berry of Company E, now U.S. Senator from Arkansas, lost a leg and was left in our hospital, which was established during the early part of the engagement.

That night we bivouacked about five miles from the battleground, resuming the retreat the next morning on the road by which we had advanced. When within a few miles of the Hatchie River, on the morning of the 5th, we heard the boom of artillery in our front. "Double quick" was the order for three or four miles, as we hurried to the assistance of our troops who were engaging the enemy, a fresh command under General _____ from Bolivar, Tennessee, who had captured and was holding the bridge across the Hatchie River on our line of retreat.

For a time the situation looked serious. A victorious army in our rear with a force of fresh troops holding the bridge, the only apparent avenue of escape, as the river was not fordable and pontoon bridges we had none. After some serious fighting near the bridge, and more or less skirmishing, marching and countermarching, in which several men of my regiment were wounded, we took a more southerly route and crossed the river on a temporary bridge hastily constructed over an old mill dam.

Tired and hungry, we continued the retreat till after dark. Our last meal, and that of crackers only, had been eaten the evening of the 3rd. Before day the next morning, by raiding a nearby sweet potato patch, I had an excellent meal of roasted potatoes. But many a poor fellow went hungry another day.

In all the engagements I had been in up to the affair at the Hatchie River, I had felt the utmost confidence in winning a victory, but when we had been double quicked about three miles and drawn up in line of battle on one side of a narrow field, with the enemy's guns just on the other side in plain view, I freely confess I had but little courage and less confidence left.

We occupied that position about 30 minutes, expecting every moment an order to charge, and feeling that I could and would obey the order, but I had no heart in the war and felt very much relieved when we quietly fell back out of range of the guns.

★ ★ ★

About the 15th of October, my regiment was detached from the 1st Missouri Brigade and ordered to Port Hudson, Louisiana. Taking the cars near Holly Springs, Mississippi, we passed through Jackson, the capital of the state, and on to _____ from which place we marched across the country to the little town on the Mississippi River bearing the name of Port Hudson. About this time, Captain Mitchell obtained a leave of absence to return home and never rejoined the command, which left me in command of the company. Port Hudson, at that time, was a village of perhaps a 150 people, mostly women and children.

Some 5,000 or 6,000 troops were in camp on our arrival. A line of earthen breastworks, some three or four miles in length with the ends resting on the river, were being constructed. The remainder of the fall and the ensuing winter were spent in drill and picket duty.

The Federals, in force, occupied Baton Rouge, some 40 miles below. Frequent skirmishes occurred during that winter and early spring. The enemy's gunboats from below paid us frequent visits, throwing shells at long range into our camps.

On the night of the 14th of May, a number of their boats essayed to pass our batteries. Two of them, the *Hartford* and *Mississippi* succeeded. The _____ was disabled, set on fire and blown up.*

A few days later, the enemy, in large force under the command of General (Nathaniel P.) Banks, occupied all of the approaches by land to Port Hudson, and with the boats in complete control of the river, cut off all communication with the outside world. By the 17th of May, their lines were advanced, after sharp skirmishing on the outside of our breastworks, to within rifle shot of most places on our line of defenses.

Batteries were soon placed in the most advantageous position that raked our lines in many places. The superiority of the enemy's guns in numbers and otherwise soon enabled them to silence our guns on the land side. In fact most of our gun carriages were shot to pieces in the course of a few days.

On the 27th of May, after heavy artillery fire from numerous batteries for two or three hours, an assault was

---

*The two ships that successfully ran the guns at Port Hudson were the *Hartford* and the *Albatross*. The *Mississippi* exploded then sank.

made on our line of works held by the 16th Arkansas and some other Arkansas troops. The enemy advanced in column of regiments four deep, across an open level field, some 500 yards in width.

Our view of the advancing columns was fine – not a single obstruction to mar the view. It was a magnificent sight, but the great odds against us looked appalling as our line was weak, averaging about one man to every five feet and no reserve force. Of one thing we felt sure, and that was that our men would do all that was possible for men to do. Every company officer, so far as I could see, stood in line with his men, musket in hand.

To facilitate rapid firing, most, if not all of the men, placed their cartridges on the works in their front. Varied were the expressions of the faces of the men. Some were serious and silent. Others joked, danced or sang short snatches of song, but there was an intense earnestness about it all. All remembered our defeat at Corinth and many remarked that we would now get even. I don't believe any doubted the result notwithstanding the disparity in numbers.

Steadily they came forward with the precision of troops on review; bristling bayonets glinting in the sunshine; above them flags fluttering in the breeze. Officers in bright uniforms on spirited horses, all made a picture long to be remembered.

In advance of their front line, perhaps 40 steps, were men carrying upright in their front, wooden boards about nine feet long and some 16 inches wide and sufficiently thick to support the weight of two or more men. Their aim was to lay these boards across the ditch in our front and thus enable the assaulting column to more easily scale our works.

When they were within about 150 yards, the order to fire was given. The front line wavered, advanced and then fell back on the second. Reforming, they again advanced to break under that withering fire and fall back the second time. By this time all the lines were more or less broken. Retiring a short distance, they again reformed and advanced the third time to be again repulsed.

After their third attempt, their broken lines took refuge in a piece of rough broken ground to their right on which the timber had been felled. From this shelter, they kept up a desultory firing on our works till dark. The assaulting columns were supported on their left by a regiment of New York Zouaves, the 165th I think, whose brilliant uniforms made a conspicuous mark for our riflemen. The enemy's loss was heavy.

Ours was light, but among our killed was Lieutenant Spain, one of my warmest personal friends. He was a general favorite and was known far and wide because of his genial happy disposition. He was brave almost to the point of recklessness. Sadly and with heavy hearts, about sunrise the next morning, we lowered his body, uncoffined, to its final resting place, to be aroused never again by beat of drum or bugle call.

After their repulse of the 27th of May, the enemy settled down to a regular siege, posting their batteries nearer and advancing their lines by means of parallels till, in some places, the lines were less than 100 feet apart. The artillery fire was almost incessant, day after day, continuing often at intervals during the night. Our guns were nearly all disabled; some of them knocked to pieces and the carriages a mess of splinters. Mortars were also posted in front of our lines, throwing shells high in the air to drop down on us. These shells were as plainly visible as a ball thrown by hand, and we were often forced to "scatter out," as the boys expressed it, to evade these unwelcome visitors.

Their gunboats from below kept up a somewhat irregular fire daily, and often at night, we could trace the course of shells as they chased one another through the air by their burning fuses, but most of their fire from their boats was directed at our shore batteries on the river and at long range doing very little damage either to men or guns.

The greatest trouble we encountered in our position came from a battery posted away to our left and beyond an angle in our works. This battery of nine inch guns raked the inside of our line of defense for quite a distance.

For protection from this raking fire, we dug trenches at right angles to our works, usually about four feet deep and about the same in width and in length from six to thirty feet. The dirt from the trenches we banked on the side from which the shells came as an additional protection. A sentry was detailed whose special duty was to watch for the smoke from these guns and seeing, he would yell out "lie down," and every mother's son would scamper to his hole in the ground, or else into some neighboring trench. At night, when not on duty, we slept in the trenches or near by so as to be able to roll in at a moment's notice.

In a short time our clothing took on the color of the yellow reddish clay of the ditches. The hot weather coupled with frequent showers made our positions everything but pleasant. In the early part of the siege, we put up what few tents we possessed for protection against the rain and the hot sun, but these were soon shot to pieces.

To add to our discomfort, especially at night, were swarms of mosquitoes that were terribly annoying. Often our faces in the morning looked like a patient just broken out with measles. As a slight protection, the boys would burn cotton or cotton rags, when they could get them, near their heads all night.

Late in the evening of May 27th, my regiment was ordered to a position about 1/2 mile north of the line we had defended that day. This position we occupied during the remainder of the siege.

At this point, our line of breastworks had been built through an old field with the timber line about 50 to 100 yards in our front. This timber, which was very heavy for about 200 yards back, had been cut down, forming a tangled mass of logs and brush. The enemy's sharpshooters took advantage of the cover thus afforded by the stumps and fallen trees and made a target of every head that showed above our works.

Every morning a detail of men was made from each company as sharpshooters for the ensuing 24 hours. For their better protection, we placed sand bags made of tents and such like material on the breastworks end to end, leaving a space five or six inches between. By placing another sack on top and over this opening, we made an excellent port hole through which our sharpshooters returned the enemy's fire. This was kept up with more or less severity day after day for weeks.

It often happened, especially of an evening, when a lull would come in firing, some fellow on one side or the other would yell out some good natured taunt or inquiry to be promptly answered by someone on the opposing side. By natural consent, all firing would cease and heads would pop up all along the line. The Yanks would get up on the logs and stumps and our fellows would stand up on the breastworks, while a mutual exchange of words took the place of shots. Often a hearty laugh from both sides would greet some pointed joke or witty retort. Neither party ever took advantage of this exposure but always gave friendly warning by calling out, "Look out over there we are going to shoot" when all parties sought shelter.

In numerous instances, Yank and Reb met on the halfway ground, under cover of darkness, to talk and exchange articles, such as sugar, coffee and tobacco. Of sugar, we had an abundance. Coffee and tobacco, we had none. In these friendly day time talks, the Yankees delighted in teasing us about our mule meat and shortage of rations generally and would tell us how they would feed us after our capture on bacon, flour bread, coffee and other things that would have been delicacies to us at that time. I mention these incidents to show that there was very little hatred or unkind feeling existing among the men on the fighting line in the regular service.

On the morning of the 14th of June, about 4:00 a.m., their batteries all along the line opened up a terrific fire, which was kept up without a moment's cessation till about daylight, when, under cover of a heavy fog, they advanced a strong force of infantry through the block of fallen timber to the edge of the old field in our front. The distance was some 50 yards in the nearest place and perhaps 100 or more at other points. We could plainly hear the command of the officers as they advanced.

Under cover of this fog, the enemy to our left, about day break, made three desperate assaults on our works. Many of them reached the ditch, but none crossed the breastworks, only as prisoners. We could plainly hear their loud huzzas mingled with the rattle of musketry as they advanced to the charge, to be answered later by the old familiar "rebel yell," gathering volume as it swept down our line.

With the lifting of the fog, the enemy in our front opened a vigorous and well directed fire on our lines. To show one's head above the breastworks would often draw the fire of several rifles. Momentarily expecting an assault, we returned the fire slowly and cautiously.

After their repulse to our left, when we felt sure they would make no further assault, we began paying attention in earnest to the gentlemen in our front. With heads for targets, a steady rifle fire was kept up by both sides till after noon when the Yanks got tired of their job and wanted to get away.

In order to do this, it was necessary to expose their bodies, more or less, as they ran from one cover to another, giving us a very great advantage that we used to the fullest. Instead of going all together and at once, they fell back at will, singly and in groups of four or five, thus giving our marksmen a great many more shots than they would have otherwise had. Many of us had shoulders bruised and sore from long continued firing that day. A Captain Cloud of my regiment loaded rifles for me so that I got a great number of shots that day.

The enemy's loss was very heavy. Ours was light comparatively, but we had a number killed and wounded. Among the killed was Lieutenant Colonel Pixlee, a splendid soldier and officer.

On the 17th of June, three days later, I went out under a flag of truce on the ground occupied by the enemy, while their dead and surviving wounded were being carried from the field by details of Confederates to designated points where they were received by the Federals. Their wounded, who fell on the 14th and were unable to get away, lay where they fell for full three days and nights in calling distance of friends. Those who survived were in a horrible condition – fly blown and wounds full of maggots. Why the Federal commander, General Banks, allowed this, I could only account for on the theory that his pride was stronger than his feeling of humanity. I feel sure that General (Franklin) Gardner, our commander, would willingly have allowed the removal of all dead and wounded if permission to do so had been asked.

Under a flag of truce, the enemy had removed their dead and wounded on May 27th, in a few hours after the battle. General Banks may have felt that it would be humiliating to ask a second time for such a favor. In fact, it was generally understood among us that General Gardner was the one who first asked for the removal of the 17th of June. This I know, the flag of truce first went out from our lines in the morning, and the removal was made later in the day. I state these facts with more particularity than I otherwise would have done because I never saw any mention made of them in any written account.

I also visited our lines to our left where the principal assaults were made. In places the dead lay in heaps. Many of them had their guns strapped on their backs, having been armed with hand grenades, which they carried one in each hand to throw over the breastworks when they should get in the ditch and then use their muskets. As stated before, a good many reached the ditch, but none crossed the breastworks only as prisoners.

In the ditch in front of one short angle of our works, I counted 27 dead men and two shaggy New Foundland dogs, who had followed their masters to death. The scent from these dead bodies, lying in that hot June sun for three days was sickening in the extreme and made the position of some of our men almost unbearable.

One morning shortly after the events narrated above, we discovered the enemy building a breastwork of sand bags at the head of a ravine in the edge of the fallen timber, about 100 yards in our front. They kept under cover, but we could see the sand bags as they were thrown up and placed in position – one after another. Steadily the work went on all day.

At night fall, Major Pittman, then in command of the regiment, called for 30 volunteers to make a sortie and destroy their works. The storming party was composed mostly of commissioned officers. Not that there was a lack of volunteers from the ranks, but because the officers insisted on going. Lieutenant (Arch S.) McKennon of Company E was placed in command.

About an hour after dark, in single file and one at a time, we silently crossed the works and, silently, advanced on the enemy's position. When we were within about 20 yards, the order to charge was given. The surprise of the Yanks was complete. They never fired a shot but ran for dear life. After partially destroying their works, we returned with three prisoners. (One was a first lieutenant of the 25th Maine Infantry.) They had hidden in the brush and were so badly scared by our first charge that they remained in hiding during our absence and were accidentally discovered on our return.

By the time our work was completed, minie balls were whistling uncomfortably close, and we were glad to reach the shelter of our breastworks. In general orders issued later, General Gardner highly complimented Lieutenant McKennon and those under him.

★ ★ ★

Our rations at the beginning of the siege were far from being good or plentiful, with the exception of sugar and molasses – of these we had an abundance. We had only a scant supply of bacon, which was soon exhausted. Beef of very poor quality was issued with more or less irregularity for about 30 days. Flour or flour bread we had none.

Corn meal made from badly weevil eaten corn was our staple of life. This becoming scarce, cow peas equally as badly weevil eaten were ground with the corn, equal parts of each. This made a compound offensive alike to taste and smell. But for weeks it was our only bread.

Sometimes ear corn was issued in lieu of this meal and was much preferred by all of us. The corn we prepared by parching or boiling.

After our beef was exhausted, horse and mule meat were issued with more or less regularity during the remainder of the siege. The flesh of these animals was fairly good though coarse grained and very poor, as they subsisted upon such vegetation as was to be found inside our breastworks. This meat we usually boiled and put over live coals to barbecue.

Wharf rats were plentiful and large, and numbers of the men killed and ate them. I tried one only. Well cooked, they might have done very well.

Having no grease of any kind, we could only boil, broil, or barbecue our meat. Parched corn or bits of parched bread was our substitute for coffee.

With this diet, and the incessant round of duties and watching, all grew more or less weak. Yet with all of these hardships, there were no words of complaint.

Our hope of relief at the beginning of the siege was not strong and had grown less as the days passed by. Still we hoped and that helped us to bear cheerfully our hardships.

★ ★ ★

With the surrender of Vicksburg July the 4th, all hope of success vanished. On the 8th of July terms of our surrender were agreed upon: Privates and noncommissioned officers to be paroled and allowed to go home. All commissioned officers to be held as prisoners.

Early on the morning of the 9th, the Confederate forces, ragged and dirty, were drawn up in line near the river bank, just south of the village of Port Hudson. After a wait of about an hour, the Federal troops with General Banks and staff at their head came in sight. General Gardner and staff rode a little in rear of General Banks and nearer our line.

With music and fluttering flags they passed, regiment after regiment, brigade after brigade, till many thousands had marched past our short line. After thousands had passed in review, a line was formed facing us when the order to ground arms was given, and we were prisoners.

A strong guard line, forming a semicircle, with each end resting on the river, confined us to an area of eight or ten acres. On the following day, the work of making out paroles

41

for the privates and noncommissioned officers was begun, and by the 13th, all of them were on their way home except the sick and wounded in the hospital. The Arkansas troops were furnished transportation by boat to points up the river.

Our battle flag, torn by shot and shell, was not surrendered but was concealed by the color bearer, Mark Buchannan, and was carried away. My old flag that I had kept all this time I gave to Sergeant Tom Parker, who concealed it in his bosom, with instructions to carry it home and give it to a member of my father's family. He sickened and died on the way, but a comrade and member of my company delivered it as requested.

In the fervor and innocence of youth, when I received that flag from the hands of my captain, I pledged myself to surrender it only with my life. When the time came that it looked like surrender, I freely confess that I did not feel like making the sacrifice of life to save my pledge.

With that old flag were entwined memories of my old home, where first its folds were unfolded to the breeze; memories of a sister and the very dear friend whose deft fingers had fashioned its stars and bars. Under its shadow had stood the dark eyed slender girl who had promised sometime to be my wife. Her hands had toyed with its fold. Fanned by the breeze, it had kissed her cheeks and dropped lovingly around her form. To me, that old flag was as dear as to a mother, the "laid away garments of her precious dead."

After the departure of the paroled men, the officers were confined to about two or three acres of ground on the river bank, embracing a few old business houses, with a double line of guards to prevent any possible chance of escape. On the morning of the 14th, we were notified that the next day we would be put aboard steamers and started north for imprisonment on Johnson's Island.

From the day of our surrender, I had hoped to escape, but so far, no feasible plan had presented itself. Lieutenant Billy Wilson (William W. Wilson) of Company E and I had talked the matter over every day, and now that we had only about 12 hours in which to make the effort, we had well nigh abandoned hope.

Late in the evening after discussing various plans, we separated with the understanding that we would meet again a little later. We had reached an agreement that in the event of an escape singly, we would go to a certain crossroads, about the center of the grounds embraced in the fortifications.

After separating from Wilson about dusk, I strolled towards the lower end of our enclosure where were situated some of the old business houses referred too. Some wagons had just been unloaded of commissary stores in one of these houses. The last one unloaded had just started out with the cover on, and the driver riding one of the four mules.

Quickly running to the hind end of the wagon, I got a glimpse of a pair of legs as they disappeared in the wagon. I lost no time in getting in and put out my hand, it was now quite dark, to find out who it was who had preceded me. The first object my hand touched was a man's heavy beard, which I recognized as that of Captain Poyner (William S.) of Company E, a warm personal friend. Not a word was spoken.

We rode only far enough to feel sure that we had passed both guard lines. Quietly crawling out, we found ourselves perhaps 50 yards past the outer guards and among 100s of Federal soldiers who thronged the streets of the village. In the darkness, our uniforms were not distinguishable from those around us, passing and touching elbows with the men on the street.

We took the road leading to the crossroads meeting place agreed upon by Lieutenant Wilson and myself – meeting and passing Federals all the way. We had some whispered talks as to our plans as we walked along. In order to appear natural and unconcerned, I attempted to whistle, but my mouth refused to perform. While we had but little hope of meeting Lieutenant Wilson, we went to the crossroads to find it occupied for quite a distance around by the tents of the enemy.

Changing our course, we soon found ourselves alone in a skirt of timbered land where we breathed a little more freely and paused long enough to exchange views as to our situation and the best way out of it. We felt sure that the Federals would have a line of guards on the breastworks, and this we yet had to pass. Once beyond that line, we would feel reasonably sure of our liberty.

A short distance to the right of the position held by my regiment during the siege, our line of breastworks crossed a ravine, about 50 feet deep and perhaps 200 feet across. In posting our guards on the breastworks, we always placed a sentry on each side of this ravine, and we reasoned that the Federals would likely place their sentries in like manner.

Entering this ravine some distance from the breastworks, we cautiously crept along till near enough to see the forms of the sentinels silhouetted against the sky on both sides. Objects down in the ravine were hardly discernable 20 feet away. Pulling off our shoes, we noiselessly crept closer, pausing every few feet to listen and to look for a sentry who might be in our front.

Finding the way clear, we were soon beyond the breastworks and out in the heavy timber and brush where we paused long enough to congratulate ourselves on our lucky escape. In the timber, it was very dark and, in many places, were dense thickets of underbrush, cane and briers. Through many of these places we had to crawl on our hands and knees, making our progress very slow. About midnight we lay down for a short rest but on account of mosquitoes it was very brief. Twice during the night we came upon cavalry outpost or pickets, but luckily discovered them in time to evade an alarm.

A short while before day, we entered some fields and felt that in this open ground we would make better progress and soon be beyond the danger line. With the first glimpse of dawn, we thought we had better seek the shelter of the timber on one side of the field.

As we entered the edge of the wood, we discovered horses tied to bushes and trees, and groups of men lying around on their blankets. Hurriedly, we made for the opposite side of the field about 1/2 mile distant. Just before reaching the fence in a piece of swampy uncleared land, we passed a large beech tree that had recently been cut down, the limbs of which were covered with the long gray moss common in that part of the country.

A moment later, a troop of cavalry came galloping along a road just outside of the fence. Hurriedly, we sought the cover of the old beech tree with its mantle of long gray moss. Ever since then, I have had a kindly feeling for that product of Dixieland. We had barely gotten under cover when bugles sounded, followed by the beat of drum on both sides of the field. To our dismay, we realized that in the darkness, we had lost our course and had wandered back into the enemy's camp.

The sun seemingly rose in the west that morning. Just over the fence, about 60 yards away, seemed to be a public road and near it a watering place of some kind where men with buckets and canteens came and went all day long. The passing of troops along the road and at the watering place was plainly visible from our hiding place. Our anxiety was intense as we feared discovery and were not certain as to consequences.

As we had sought shelter in different parts of the tree, we spoke not a word during the day as we feared to make the least noise or change our positions. Lack of food and water gave us but little concern. As the hours passed, we began to take hope.

When good dark came, I crawled out of my hiding place and went around to where Captain Poynor had sought shelter to find his legs from the knees down in plain view. When quite dark, we ventured out, cautiously picking our way, near the center of the field both sides of which were lighted up by camp fires.

About a mile from our starting place, we came to a lane and heard a squad of infantry passing. Listening, we found they were posting guards along the lane. Crawling up near the fence, we waited perhaps half an hour. For a time, they walked their beats, exchanging a few words when they met.

Presently the walking ceased. One struck a match and lighted a pipe; another made a noise by bringing his gun to an order. By this means we located the position of the two sentries nearest us and some 40 or 50 yards apart. With shoes in our hands, we cautiously climbed the fence, crossed the road and the other fence without being discovered.

While in the open ground with the North Star to guide us, it was easy to keep our direction; but we soon struck the timber where we encountered the same trouble experienced the night before, darkness and tangled thickets through which we had to crawl with the added fear of again losing our direction. With the exception of a short rest about midnight we traveled all night.

Just before daylight, we heard chickens crowing in our front and a little to our left. Knowing the people of the country were in full sympathy with the Cause of the South, we concluded to go to this house for information as to our whereabouts and to get something to eat.

Approaching the house from the back side, we found a Negro woman drawing water from a well in the yard. In answer to our questions, she said a Doctor Mills lived there and that he was at home. We requested her to tell him that we would like to see him, which she did.

In a few minutes, the doctor came out when we explained our situation. He was a man about 50 years of age and of very pleasing address. He greeted us cordially and told us we were then just five and one quarter miles from Port Hudson, and just one quarter of a mile beyond the enemy's cavalry outposts, which were plainly visible from the road in front of the house. We felt like traveling, but the good doctor said there was no danger, that we must stay for breakfast and he would keep watch, and so we concluded to stay, but we kept a sharp lookout along that road.

We sat down to a breakfast that morning, the like of which we had not seen for many a day. In fact it was the first meal I had eaten in a private home for over twelve months. Before leaving, the doctor took out his pocket book and said, "If you gentlemen need money, my purse is at your service." With feelings of gratitude we bade him good-bye.

Following his directions across the country and avoiding all public roads, we were soon practically free from danger. About noon, we met a Confederate scout and felt safe and free once more. At a number of farm houses we were met with the most cordial reception, with offers of food, fruit, melons, etc.

I will here state that my friend Lieutenant Wilson succeeded in getting away that night by getting in possession of part of a Federal uniform and impersonating a Federal officer. In the same manner Captain (Jesse L) Cravens of my regiment also escaped.

Eight other officers of my regiment succeeded in getting away before reaching prison. Most of them by jumping overboard while going up the Mississippi River and swimming ashore. Among those who escaped by jumping overboard and swimming ashore, I recall now, the following: Lt. George Crump of Co._____(E),  Lieutenant  William McConnell of Co. _____(C). Lieutenant Nigh (Hezekiah) Blackard (Co. A), Captain Dan Boone of Co. I, Lieutenant Billy (William R.) Lawson, Co. I. There were others whose names I cannot now remember. A Lieutenant (David C.) Meadows of the 14th Arkansas lost his life by drowning in the attempt.

After reaching a point of safety, some 25 miles from Port Hudson, we turned our steps in the direction of home, some 500 or 600 hundred miles distant. The next day we overtook Lieutenant J.H. Berry of my regiment, now a U.S. Senator from Arkansas, who had lost a leg at Corinth on October 4, 1862, and had followed the regiment to Port Hudson. He spent most of the time with friends, some distance out in the country, where he remained during the siege.

With him was a younger brother, Billy Berry, under 16 years of age, who had been discharged from the service a short time before the beginning of the siege, but who voluntarily remained to take part in the defense of the place. Having his discharge papers, he was permitted by the Federals to go at will.

Lieutenant Berry had hired a one horse conveyance to carry him and his brother to a point on the Mississippi River, some 75 miles distant and above Port Hudson about the same distance. Glad of the company of our friends and of our lucky escape, we tramped cheerfully over the dusty roads.

As a rule, the people on the way were very kind and seldom charged us for meals or lodgings. We crossed the river at old Fort Adams in a skiff and in sight of one of the enemy's gunboats. Occasionally, we could get conveyance for short distances, but we walked by far the greater part of the way. Of course we had to get conveyance for Berry all the way.

At Little Rock, Arkansas, we separated. Berry and his brother going up the river to Ozark where their father then resided. Captain Poynor and I continuing our journey afoot, across the country. When within about 75 miles of home, we had the good fortune to get horses from friends and rode the balance of the way.

★ ★ ★

On our arrival at home, we found that most of the paroled men had preceded us by a few days. Several had sickened and died on the way. The condition of the country at this time was comparatively quiet, though it had been overrun a number of times by Federal troops, and was yet subject to raiding parties from Missouri on the north and the mountain country lying to the south.

We soon found that paroles were disregarded by Federal soldiers as was evidenced by a company of Federals from Missouri under the command of one Captain Jim Moore, who killed in cold blood several men of my regiment.

On the same raid, they captured and killed my former Captain E.G. Mitchell (Co. D. 16th Arkansas). The killing was brutally done in the presence of his wife and child after he had surrendered and given up his arms. The killing of Mitchell occurred about day break; he having been surprised at his home on the morning of September the 27th.

Hurriedly, a party was organized and started in pursuit. These men were poorly armed and short of ammunition, but they were in fighting mood. The pursued and the pursuing party numbered about one hundred men each. About midnight of the following night, we came upon their camp, situated in some lots, enclosed by an old fashioned staked and ridered fence, in which were situated a number of log stables, cribs, etc. We dismounted about one half mile away and made the assault on foot.

The enemy took shelter in and around the cribs and stables and after a sharp engagement, lasting perhaps ten or fifteen minutes, the assaulting party was forced to retire, but not until their ammunition was practically exhausted. Many of the men had only four to six rounds.

After the first fire, everybody in the darkness acted according to his own impulse. Sanguine of victory, I rushed forward to the lot fence, reloading a double barreled shotgun as I went. Just over the fence, the forms of several Federal soldiers rose up. I called out "Surrender." The answer was a pistol ball fired through a crack in the fence, striking me in the left breast just below the nipple.

Taking hold of the fence, I let myself down on the ground. The pain was not intense as many would suppose, but a feeling of numbness followed that rendered me practically helpless but without any impairment of mental faculties, so far as I can now recall. Several of my comrades came up in a few moments. To one of them I gave my gun.

Mr. Mose Holmes, a neighbor, offered to carry me to a place of safety, but feeling that my wound was mortal, I declined. Some of the boys threw down the lot fence near me, and took out a number of the enemy's horses. In a short time the firing ceased, and I knew we had been beaten. I could plainly hear the Federals talking.

I now thought of my situation more intently perhaps than I had done while the fighting was going on. Feeling of my wound, I found that the ball had ranged slightly down, coming out at my back about three inches to the left of the spinal column. It was bleeding freely at both places, and I felt that I had but a short time to live.

More than once the thought occurred to me that, perhaps, this is a dream from which I will presently awaken. As well as I can now recall my feelings, after a lapse of over forty years, I had no fear or dread of death. My greatest regret was the thought that I would die alone, and none would ever know how I died. I thought of my belief on religious matters, having been an agnostic for a number of years, but felt not the slightest desire to change my views. I had absolutely no fear of the hereafter.

How long I lay there with these and other thoughts passing rapidly through my mind, I have but little idea. Thoughts of the old home and the home folks with the grief I knew they would feel. Thoughts of inexpressible tenderness for the dark eyed girl that I so dearly loved.

Remembering the brutality of these Federals, I had no desire to fall into their hands, and I pondered some time before I decided to call for help. They were only a few steps away and their voices were plainly audible. Finally I called to them. No answer came to my call, but in a few minutes I heard the footsteps of a man approaching slowly and cautiously along the fence. When, in a few feet, he asked me who I was and what I was doing there. I told him my name and that I was badly wounded. Stepping a little nearer, without a word, he presented a pistol to my face and snapped it once or twice, but it failed to fire.

Realizing his intentions I begged him to spare my life. His only answer, as he unstrapped a carbine from his shoulder, was, "Oh yes, god damn you." I felt the force of one blow above my eyes.

When I regained consciousness, I was alone and all around was quiet. Again the thought came to me that I was dreaming and that I would soon wake up. When fully aroused, I found that my boots were gone and a sword belt that I prized very highly as it once belonged to Lieutenant Bush of my company who was killed or died of wounds received at Corinth, Mississippi. The wounds about my head and hands (I had evidently thrown up my hands to word off the blow) were far more painful than my gunshot wound.

Expecting no mercy at the hands of these men and hearing their voices again close by, I decided to attempt to crawl away. In my first effort, I succeeded in going several steps, crawling on my hands and knees when I fainted. Recovering consciousness I repeated the effort several times, fainting after each attempt. How far I crawled, I have but little idea, probably not over 50 yards.

In my last effort, I came in contact with a wounded Confederate soldier named Harrison. He was suffering from a gun wound through the fleshy part of the thigh. We carried on a whispered conversation concerning our wounds and our situation generally. At the same time, lying as close together as possible, "spooning" as the boys termed it, for the warmth we derived from each others bodies. In the cold night air, with the loss of blood, we were thoroughly chilled. How long we lay there, I now have but little idea, but think from one to two hours.

Finally, we heard a number of men approaching through the bush talking in low tones. When within a few feet of us and realizing that discovery was certain and being a Master Mason, I uttered the words of distress, known to all members of the order.

In answer, I heard one of the party say: "I know him. He is a gentleman." There was kindness in the tone of his voice that my ears were quick to detect; that gave me some assurance of protection. I also recognized the voice as that of a man named Towne Hopper; a man I had known very well prior to the breaking out of the war and who lived only a few miles from my father's home. He was a Mason.

With the care and tenderness of a brother, he helped to carry us to a nearby house where he made pallets of blankets, before an open fire place, built a fire to warm us, gave us water and otherwise administered to our wants, so far as lay in his power. But for his influence, we would doubtless have shared the same fate as the other unfortunates who had fallen into their hands the day previous.

Another factor in my favor was the belief that my wounds were mortal and that I could only live a short time. I overheard some of them say: "He won't last much longer" and such like expressions, while I shared the same belief because at that time I thought a shot through the lungs meant certain death.

I rather wanted them to think I was sure to die and managed to breathe a little harder because I was not certain as to whether they would let me die of my present wounds or aid my exit to the next world by additional ones. I had no doubt as to the friendship of my friend Hopper, but I knew there were men in the party who would not hesitate to commit any act of cruelty.

Just before daybreak the Federals left, leaving us with the woman of the house who treated us with scant courtesy. Her husband was in the Federal Army.

A little after daybreak, a troop of Confederates galloped up to the house, among them my brother W.W. Bailey. After their repulse, they had fallen back about a half mile where they remained till morning. I have often thought that my brother suffered more from mental anguish that night than I did from my bodily wounds. He was one of the assaulting party but only learned of my being wounded when they retired to their horses.

The troop only remained a few minutes, leaving with the understanding that they would return as speedily as possible with conveyances and move us to our homes, about 30 miles distant. Some neighboring women, a Miss Goforth and a Miss Erwin, came in during the day and were very kind and attentive, staying all day and the following night.

About daybreak the next morning, the clatter of horse hoofs announced the return of the party with conveyances for our removal. With them came two unexpected visitors in the persons of my sister and the dark eyed girl, who was dearer than all beside. Taking a seat by my pallet on the floor, she placed one hand in mine, and with the other smoothed back the tangled locks from my forehead, looking the love her lips need not speak. In her presence, the desire to live grew strong, and I think aided materially in my recovery.

No time was lost by my scout friends, consisting of about one dozen men, in placing us in the "carryall" drawn by a single horse and starting on our return journey. The roads were very rough and in places full of small boulders that made the ride a very painful one. But the presence of one dearly loved, who was also the driver, enabled me to bear with fortitude, and, I think, may add with a feeling of genuine pleasure the long tedious ride that September day. With the exception of a few slight hemorrhages, no ill effects from the ride resulted. My wounded comrade, Harrison, grew rapidly worse and was left at a farm house on the way, where he died a day or two later.

About sunset we reached my father's home, much to the relief of all of us. A day or two later a severe hemorrhage set in, when the attending physician, a Dr. Robertson, told me I had only a short time to live. The announcement was something of a shock at first, as I had been feeling very hopeful, but I soon accepted with a spirit of resignation what I thought was the inevitable. I mention this to show how readily we can adjust ourselves to the inevitable.

Following that hemorrhage of the lungs, I felt perfectly easy and soon fell asleep; to awaken several hours later with the feeling that I was going to get well. From that time on, hemorrhages grew less frequent and lighter, and at the end of 30 days from the time I received my wounds, I was in the saddle, feeling none the worse from my experience, except that I had not fully regained my strength.

★ ★ ★

During the time of my convalescence, the paroled men of my command had been gathered and ordered to join the Confederate forces in Southern Arkansas.

In the meantime, the Federal forces had captured Little Rock and established posts at various points on the Arkansas River, as far west as Fort Smith; making it very dangerous to pass their lines with a small force, such as I would have been able to get together. For this reason, I remained inside the Federal lines till the following April.

I frankly admit that I was not sorry that I had such reasons, as my inclination to remain was very strong. There were a few Confederate soldiers in the country; mostly members of independent commands from North Arkansas and Missouri.[3]

Most of these men preferred the free but more hazardous life of independent soldier and scout to the irksome duties of the regularly organized forces of the Confederate Army. As occasion required, these men would form companies ranging in numbers from a corporal's guard to 50 or more. As a rule, they were well mounted, superb horsemen and experts with pistols, their main reliance in action.

The character of warfare carried on along the border, where quarter was seldom being asked or given, developed a type of desperate fighters, equal perhaps to any of like character, the world ever produced.

There was practically no attempt at discipline. Every man went and came at his own sweet will; but all obeyed with promptness the order of their chosen officer while on duty. When assembled for offensive or defensive purposes, they selected for the particular object in view one or more commanders from among those best fitted to command. That honor was often conferred on the writer.

A decided majority of the people of the northern tier of counties in Arkansas were Confederates or in sympathy with the Confederate Cause. The mountain counties to the south were dominated by Union men, mostly deserters from the Confederate Army. The southern counties of Missouri were strongly Union in sentiment.

---

[3]Shortly after my recovery from my wounds, a company of about 60 mounted men was organized of which I was elected captain, John Cecil, first lieutenant, and Fielding Wilburn, second lieutenant. Later, owing to the difficulty of obtaining food for ourselves and feed for our horses, we disbanded and formed smaller groups.

Thus situated, we were subject to numerous raiding parties from Missouri on the north and the mountain country to the south. Most of these raids were made more for plunder than to wage war on armed men. Horses and cattle were the booty mostly sought, but household goods, such as clothes, bed clothing and, in fact, anything of value were also carried off. As a result of these raids many were killed on both sides, among them quite a number of non-combatants, old men and boys in their teens.

★ ★ ★

The first invasion by any considerable force in the latter part of 1863 was by a battalion of cavalry with one piece of artillery, commanded by a Major (John I.) Worthington. This command was known as the 1st Arkansas Cavalry and was made up in good part by deserters from the Confederate Army. We gave them such a warm reception that they were glad to escape under cover of darkness, leaving a number of dead and wounded as well as their wagon train.

In connection with this affair, I will state that in looking over the official records of the war, I found a report of this raid by Major Worthington in which he states that he inflicted a heavy loss on the Confederates, when, as a matter of fact, we suffered no loss, either in killed or wounded. I mention this to show the unreliability of the reports of many officers.

About this time, a party of raiders visited my father's house one night. While in and about the house, my mother stepped out on a gallery in front of the house and rang a bell for the purpose of making them believe that a force of Confederates was nearby, and that the ringing of the bell was a signal they would understand. One of the party, a man named Guy, well known to the family, kicked her off of the gallery, from which she sustained injuries that confined her to her bed for some time. The ringing of the bell, however, had the desired effect as they left at once.

Shortly after this occurrence, a small party of Confederates struck a fresh trail of Federal raiders, which we could easily follow as the ground was soft from recent rain. From the freshness of their horse tracks, we knew they were only a short distance ahead of us. Pressing forward, we found where they had fed their horses from a nearby cornfield. Here the raiders divided.

Following the trail of one party, we overtook them about a mile away where they had stopped at a Union man's house for dinner. Three of the party were killed and one taken prisoner. Among the killed was the man Guy, who had so brutally assaulted my mother only a few days before.

The one prisoner taken, fortunately for him, fell into my hands, as he would likely have been killed by any other of the party, as he was unknown to them. I knew him well and believed him to be an honorable, upright man, notwithstanding the fact that some of his companions were bad. His father's family was warm personal friends of mine and near neighbors of my father. Two of his brothers were in the Southern Army.

To show that I was not mistaken in my estimate of the man, (Crump was his name) I will relate the following incidents. With the prisoner, we immediately returned to the field where they had fed their horses and took up the trail of the other party. This trail we followed till darkness compelled us to abandon it. Knowing that a Union family lived some miles ahead, we pushed on to that place hoping to find the party there.

When within a quarter of a mile of the house, we dismounted, tied our horses in the woods and approached the house on foot; the prisoner going with us. I required a pledge from him that he would not attempt to escape, and that if we got separated in the darkness, he would report back to where our horses were tied. We captured two Federals in the house, but not of the party we had been pursuing. Crump had not only the opportunity to escape in the darkness but could have taken one or more of our horses as they were left without a guard. The next day I gave him permission to go to his father's home, where he remained some two weeks.

A few days later, I took dinner with him at his father's. While there, we saw a drove of wild turkeys nearby. Giving him a pistol, which, by the way, was one of a pair I had taken from him when he surrendered, we went out together to try our luck at turkey shooting. He got two or three shots but missed.

My first and only shot brought down a fine gobbler. I think that one shot, which was a very fine one, but quite accidental, gave him a very exaggerated idea of my marksmanship. Shortly after this, learning that some Confederates had threatened to kill him if he remained longer in the country, I took a couple of men and escorted him some 30 miles towards Missouri where he was entirely out of danger and bid him good-bye.

I often heard of him and from him and, on several occasions, exchanged shots with the Federal scouts when he was one of the party, but I never met him again.

★ ★ ★

An amusing incident occurred one day about this time while scouting through the country. There was a Union family named Jones, who lived a few miles from my father and with whom I was very well acquainted. Jones belonged to the Union army, and, from some cause, we had reasons for believing that he and a troop of Federal soldiers were hiding somewhere in the country, and we were very anxious to come up with them. Most of our party, about 20 in number, were dressed in Federal uniform. As Mrs. Jones knew me very well, we conceived the idea of going to the Jones house with me as a prisoner and the men in Federal uniform as my captors. The scheme was a success so far as deceiving Mrs. Jones was concerned. Her husband with a scout of Federals were in the country, but she was ignorant of their whereabouts at that time.

Assuming as best I could the role of a prisoner doomed to be speedily put to death, I asked her to intercede for me and say a word on my behalf, which she promised in a half hearted way to do. The boys related to her gleefully the circumstances of my capture, and, from her manner, it was easy to see that she was delighted over the fact that I was a prisoner. While pretending a friendship for me in my presence, she gave the boys to understand that I was no saint and richly deserved the fate that she felt was in store for me.

While at the house, some of the boys made mention that they had had nothing to eat for the last 24 hours. Mrs. Jones most cheerfully went in the house and took from under a feather bed a great number of pies and cakes, which she was evidently saving for her husband and friends, and distributed them among her supposed friends, forgetting to offer any to the prisoner.

The play now was getting serious for me because I wanted some of those pies and cakes and wanted them badly, but I was playing prisoner and couldn't say a word. Finally some of the boys suggested giving the prisoner something to eat, but this raised a storm of protest from some of them, who said it would be a "waste of victuals" and let the "damned Rebel go hungry." Finally the prisoner got his share and we rode away.

I learned afterwards that Mrs. Jones, as soon as we left, hurried over to a neighbor's house, friends of mine, to tell the news of my capture; where she learned to her great discomfiture that she had given her pies and cakes to the hated Rebels. If the good Saint Peter requires forgiveness for all the wrongs done us in this world as a condition precedent to entering the "Pearly Gates," I am afraid Mrs. Jones will never enter therein.

★ ★ ★

The winter of '63 and '64 was noted for the extremely cold weather and the amount of snow that fell. As we seldom dared to sleep in houses, one might think that we suffered much from cold; but such was not the case. As a rule we were very well clothed and most every man had two or more blankets captured from the Federals. By two or more sleeping together we were usually quite comfortable.

Our time was spent in scouting more or less during the day, till long after dark, sometimes on the hunt of an enemy but very often to evade him. When we wished to stop for the night, we usually selected some secluded place in the woods, first supplying ourselves with feed for our horses from some field or corn crib, where we would build a fire in a ravine or some depression in the ground, from which the light of our camp fire could be seen only a short distance away. When the enemy was in force, and we knew they were nearby, we always left our campfires and slept elsewhere.

We seldom kept a guard but all would lie down to sleep with their horse tied close by. We soon found that our horses could detect the approach of any unusual object in the darkness, at much greater distance and more quickly than we were able to do. In various ways, they gave warnings of any unusual happenings. A slight snort, uneasy movements or a listening attitude always called for investigation.

From incessant watching both day and night, it took but a slight noise to arouse us from sleep. When morning came, we would usually go to some nearby farm house for breakfast and always felt sure of a welcome. If quite a number were in the party, we would divide and go to different places; to meet again at some designated point. On many occasions we went hungry, sometimes missing several meals in succession.

To feed and groom our horses was our first care, as our lives often depended on their speed and endurance. That we became very much attached to our horses, under the circumstances, was natural. Had it been necessary, we would cheerfully have gone hungry to feed them. Knowing the country, however, and the people as we did, we usually had but little trouble in getting something to eat for ourselves and horses.

I was the owner of a dark bay horse, one I had captured from a Federal in the early part of the winter and whom I named Wild Bill. He was one of medium size, fleet of foot, a splendid saddler and endowed with wonderful powers of endurance. To say that I became strongly attached to Wild Bill is but a mild expression of my feelings toward him. And I somehow felt that he had in a limited degree, at least, a fondness for me. But for his speed and endurance on several occasions, this story would not have been written.

In the latter part of '64, while serving with the infantry, I sold him, and the last time I saw him, he was doing service in the field artillery in Southern Arkansas. Not withstanding the intervening 40 years between then and now, there is yet a warm place in my heart for Wild Bill. In after years, when I was the owner of a well filled barn, I often thought what a pleasure it would be to feed and care for my faithful horse in his old age.

Reverting back to the severity of the winter and the danger of sleeping in houses, I will relate the following incident. In the early part of January 1864, some of the boys had arranged for a dance one night at a neighboring house a few miles from my father's home. There were about a dozen boys and about an equal number of girls in attendance. The snow was ten or twelve inches deep and the night bitterly cold.

After spending some time with them, I concluded to go home and spend the remainder of the night with the home folks. All had retired for the night sometime before my arrival. Tying my horse out some distance from the house, I went in and lay down on a pallet before the fire and was soon sound asleep.

Suddenly the tramp, tramp of feet going around the house in the dry powdery snow awoke me. Listening a moment, I felt sure the house was being surrounded by Federals. Feeling that I had been caught like a rat in a trap and believing that death was the penalty, I leave to the reader to imagine my feelings.

The noise had awakened all the family and made upon their minds the same impression, but all kept perfectly quiet. Cautiously pulling the door slightly ajar, I saw to my inexpressible relief cattle instead of Federal soldiers. A gate in front of the house had in some way been opened, and the cattle came in, some going one way, and some the other around the house.

I think that was the worst scare I had during the four years of war. For some time after that, I preferred the shadows of the deep woods to the shelter of a house, regardless of the weather. A house is liable to be surrounded at any time, and many lives were lost in that way by parties venturing to sleep in their homes.

During the fall and early winter, I had as an almost constant companion, Billy Berry (Private William. D. Berry, Co. E, 16th Arkansas) having been discharged at Port Hudson on account of being under 16 years of age. He was far above the average in intelligence and was a most companionable youth. For sometime, we had shared the same rations and slept under the same blankets. He was brave, generous and true, and I was very fond of him, and he was devotedly attached to me.

With a company of about 50 men, under a captain named (John) Cecil, we were scouting in the mountains south of us on the hunt of the Federals who frequently made jayhawking raids through the Crooked Creek Valley. I was in command of the advance guard of seven or eight men, when late in the evening of the first day out, a Federal, well mounted and well armed, showed himself in the road about 150 yards in advance, waving a pistol over his head. We immediately gave chase.

After a run of about one mile, Wild Bill was close enough for me to take a shot, when the Federal threw up his hands and called out that he would surrender. Some of the boys wanted to kill him, and I had to threaten to shoot one young fellow, whose mother's house had been robbed by this man in order to save him from instant death. With us at the time was a brother of the captured man. Thus it often happened that brothers met on opposing sides.

In the afternoon of the second day as we were advancing up a valley, a Federal mounted on a gray horse came meeting us. When within about 100 yards, he wheeled and put spurs to his horse. We gave chase, when after a short run, he quit the road and led us along the foot of a very steep rugged hill, heavily timbered. We were gradually lessening the distance between us, when to our left and a little in front, not over 50 yards away, we saw a company of dismounted men, 21 in number, waiting to receive us.

There were only seven of us in the pursuing party, but every man reined his horse's head in the direction of the enemy and opened fire, which was promptly returned. Bullets from the rifles of these mountain men flew thick and close. My young friend Berry, who sat his horse only a few feet away, called to me saying he was shot and asked me to take him from his horse.

Dismounting, I took him in my arms and laid him down behind a tree. Rolling over he continued firing at the enemy, who were now retreating. By this time the welcome sound of horse feet told us that our friends were coming. Owing to the steepness of the hill and the rough nature of the ground, most of the Federals escaped. Four were killed and one taken prisoner. Most of their arms and all of their horses, 21 in number, were captured.

Returning from the chase, I found my young friend lying where I had left him. Bending over him to change his position, he put his arms around my neck, looked up in my face and said: "I love you." Words are inadequate to express my feelings at that moment. And after these long years, the memory of that incident touches my heart with the deepest emotion.

Knowing that the end was near, yet he uttered no word of complaint and scarcely a groan escaped his lips. He met the last enemy, death, like he had met the enemies of his country, bravely and fearlessly. Among the hills of North Arkansas, in the Crooked Creek Valley, the "boy soldier" is "sleeping his manhood away." But his memory will ever be dear to me.

As an evidence of the close shooting of these mountain men, I will state that in addition to the wound received by my young friend, his horse was also shot and a ball passed through a coat tied behind his saddle. My brother L.W. Bailey, who was one of the party, had his horse severely wounded, and three separate balls pierced his clothing. Others of the party had marks of bullets through their clothing.

The names of the men not mentioned, who were in the advance guard on this occasion, were Ben Adair (Private B. F. Adair, Co. D, 16th Arkansas), James Parker (Sergeant, Co. E, 16th Arkansas), Irvin Beller (Co. D, 16th Arkansas), and

Guinn Deering (possibly Q. M. Dearing, Co. D, Harrell's Cavalry Battalion)

About the 20th of January, 1864, a strong force of Federal cavalry, three regiments with artillery, swept down through the Crooked Creek Valley and established camps at Marshall's Prairie in the eastern part of Carroll County. A small party of Confederates, 12 in number, concluded that we would reconnoiter their camps and at least exchange a few shots with them. We were well mounted and well armed and felt a good deal of confidence in ourselves.

As we neared their camp, we were joined by a man named Gibson and his son, who was probably 18 years of age. They were armed and well mounted and were evidently going to join the Federals. But at the time, we had no suspicion as to their intentions.

As we drew nearer to the enemy's camp, now about a mile away, Gibson and his son still with us, we were suddenly confronted by a scout of Federals – 75 or 100 strong. We got the exchange of shots all right, and, in addition, a three mile run for dear life with the enemy in hot pursuit. After a run of perhaps a mile, the elder Gibson halted, evidently to surrender, but was killed at once. A few days later the young man joined the Federals.

My brother L.W. Bailey (Private, Co. I, 27th Arkansas) received a slight wound in the shoulder, and all of us got such a scare that we didn't go on a hunt for the enemy without taking some thought with regard to numbers.

From this camp, the Federals sent out scouts in all directions and in such force that our only safety lay in keeping out of the way or in flight as we could not hope to win against such odds. Another factor against us was the fact that if man or horse was disabled, death was almost certain as very few prisoners were taken.

After occupying this camp at Marshall's Prairie (present day Western Grove) for some time, they moved to Bellefonte and later to the Klepper Mill on Crooked Creek, about three miles from my father's home. Led by Union men who lived in the country and who knew every path as well as I did, they scouted over every hill and valley, woodland and mountain, till one place was no more secure than another.

For over two months, we seldom missed hearing their morning bugle call, and scarcely a day passed that we were not in sight of some scouting party. The trail of their scouting parties were to be found in all directions. We could easily tell the trail of a Federal scout from that of the Confederates. Usually their horses were larger than ours and the size of the tracks was one sign, but the sign we relied on mainly was the eight nails in a shoe used by them, where we used only six in shoeing our horses.

For weeks this scouting was kept up till most of the Confederates were either killed or driven out of the country. A full record of the events that occurred in the Crooked Creek Valley and the adjacent country during the months of January, February, March and April 1864, would fill many volumes.

There were many acts of barbarous cruelty. Sick and wounded men were dragged out of their beds and brutally murdered in the presence of their families. House burning was of almost daily occurrence. It was no unusual sight to see from some elevated point in the country smoke ascending from burning homes in widely separated locations at the same time.

During the latter part of the winter and early spring, probably half the houses in the Crooked Creek Valley were burned, and their occupants – mostly women and children – driven to seek shelter elsewhere. This was often in stables and cribs or in rail pens, hastily constructed by the women and larger children as a partial protection from the inclemency of the weather. Thus the greatest hardships of the war fell upon old age – women and children. That the enemy paid in human life a heavy toll is evidenced by the numerous graves scattered over a wide expanse of country, where sleep men who wore the blue.

Some time in the latter part of the winter, a party of six Confederates discovered a Federal Scout of probably a 100 men with about a dozen wagons foraging at a neighbor's house. Knowing the route they would take on the return to camp, we took a favorable position on the road with the view of firing on them from ambush.

We had been in position a short time when we saw two officers of the command galloping leisurely along the road, some distance in advance of the main body. We let them pass but quickly mounted our horses that were tied a short distance in our rear, and, by taking a short cut through the woods, rode into the road a short distance behind them. They were still riding in a gallop and never discovered our presence till we were in 30 steps or less.

To our summons to halt and surrender, they cast one glance behind them and put spurs to their horses. On the first fire one man and horse went down. The other rode perhaps 50 yards when a bullet from my pistol, not over three feet from the rider, brought him to the ground. I secured his arms, a very fine Remington pistol and a new hat richly adorned with ostrich plumes, which I felt was quite a "feather in my cap."

By this time the advance guard of the enemy was in sight and we beat a hasty retreat. They gave no pursuit but loaded their dead on their wagons and went on their way. One of the men killed was named Cross, a lieutenant in the Quartermaster's Department. The other one was a first lieutenant in Company E, 2nd Arkansas Cavalry and was named Henry C. Kelly.

Only a few days prior to this affair (March 25, 1864) this man Kelly had, in a boastful brutal way, said to my sweetheart, Miss Baines, whose home was nearby, "We will get your Rebel captain some of these days and put his head on a pole." Such is the fortune of war. He fell at my hands, and, after 40 years, my head occupies its accustomed place.

My sweetheart's home was in a very public place and only five miles from the enemy's camp, and their scouts were passing and repassing nearly every day. Notwithstanding the danger, I made numerous calls, sometimes at night but often in the day time. I made brief calls, but always keeping a sharp lookout for the enemy.

A few days after the incident narrated above, I concluded to call early one morning. In company with seven others, we had spent the night previous within a couple of miles of her father's home. So leaving the boys where we had spent the night, I rode off alone with the understanding that I would return in a short time. I found my sweetheart at a neighbor's house about a mile away from her home.

For greater security, we walked out along an unfrequented road about 100 yards from the house, took a seat on a fallen tree and were quietly talking of the many things of interest to us; blissfully forgetting for the time being, the dreadful state of affairs by which we were surrounded. We had been seated but a few minutes when something attracted the attention of my horse.

Looking in the direction indicated, the woods looked blue with Federal Cavalry about 70 yards away, riding straight towards us. For a moment, I think I stood perfectly still, paralyzed with fear. "Run, run," from the lips of the white faced girl by my side broke the spell. Amid a shower of bullets, I mounted my horse and the race for life began.

My horse was more or less jaded from recent hard riding, and I soon found that a number of them were gaining on me. Once my horse ran against a sapling in the thick woods that brought him nearly to a standstill and, a moment later, an over-hanging limb nearly unhorsed me. I had ridden perhaps a quarter of a mile, not fully recovered from my fright, with the foremost of my pursuers not over 30 yards behind and shooting at every jump, when for the first time I thought of my arms. Turning in my saddle I fired twice. The report of my pistol restored confidence and made me feel equal to any emergency.

Looking back after my two shots, I saw the enemy had halted, and a horse with an empty saddle was running away at full speed. Believing that I had at least wounded one of their numbers, I felt jubilant. As I afterward learned, one of my shots had struck the leader – a man named Watkins – in the shoulder and knocked him from his horse.

About a mile away, I met my friends, who had heard the firing, and, suspecting that I was in trouble, were coming to my assistance. After the Federals had given up the pursuit, they returned to the house and taunted my sweetheart with statements to the effect that they had killed her lover. Crump, the man whom I had once captured and befriended and who was one of the party, quietly told her the facts.

Miss Baines had picked up one of my gloves that I had dropped in mounting my horse. One of the soldiers, more brutal than the others, snatched it from her hand. In the run, I lost my fine feathered hat, and, for some time after, my only headwear was a bandana handkerchief worn turban fashion. A week or so later in passing over this ground, I found my hat where I had lost it in the thick brush, but mice or something of that kind had cut off all the fine feathers.

The Federals soon took up our trail, burning the house nearest the place where we had camped the previous night. The ground being very soft from recently melted snow, our trail was easily followed as we made no attempt to conceal it as we often did by scattering and coming together again at some designated point. The following night, which was a very stormy one, we camped within a quarter of a mile of each other, neither party being aware of the close proximity of the other.

Early the next morning, some of the boys rode to the nearest house, about a quarter of a mile away, to get breakfast, and found the enemy in possession of the house and premises. After feeding our horses and getting breakfast at a house some two miles away, we leisurely traveled through the neighborhood, making a circuit of three or four miles, returning to the road traveled an hour or two earlier. Finding they had not passed in pursuit, we concluded they had given up the hunt.

Anxious to learn something of their whereabouts, we took the back trail over the road we had traveled earlier in the day. We had ridden but a short distance when we saw them coming around a short turn in the road about 75 yards away. We saw them first and got the first fire, which they promptly returned, but showed no disposition to advance till we retreated.

After a short run we halted and gave them another round. Again they halted, notwithstanding they out-numbered us eight or ten to one. A running fight of a mile or more ensued, in which one of our party, Jack Thomas*, a splendid soldier was killed, his horse having failed him.

A short time after this occurrence, on a moonlight night, a party of Federal raiders from the mountains to the south made a jayhawking raid through part of the Crooked Creek Valley; robbing a number of homes and returning booty laden to their homes in the mountains. This occurred in the early part of the night, and it so happened that two or three small parties of Confederates – numbering all toll about 25 men – were near by.

Word was quickly passed around, and we were soon on their trail, which we could follow easily in the bright moonlight, as they took a plain traveled road on their return trip. We followed their trail about 18 miles, arriving in the neighborhood of their homes just as the moon went down – an hour or so before dawn.

With the break of day we were on the move, the main body under Captain Cecil going up a valley, where lived a number of known Union men, whom we had reason for

---

*Possibilities include: James Thomas, Co. F., 16th Arkansas; John Tomas, Co., D, 16th Arkansas; John Thomas, Co. I., 16th Arkansas; or John H. Thomas, Co. K., 16th Arkansas.

believing were among the raiders. With three men, Maris Trotter, Carl Wellborn and James Adder (Private, Co. F, 16th Arkansas), I went up a smaller valley where other Union men lived, with high steep rugged hills on either side. By this time it was broad daylight.

After going a short distance, we discovered two Federals on top on one of the hills to our right. Both were afoot, but one was leading a horse. They were 300 or 400 hundred yards away, and we saw that they had not discovered us. Riding close up to the foot of the hill and out of their sight, we began the ascent along a narrow winding trail – riding single file. I was in front, and, as we neared the crest of the hill, suddenly from behind a big tree – not over 30 feet away – a man leveled a double barreled shot gun, calling out, "Who are you?" "Surrender," was our answer.

As his gun came in range, with my body I dropped by the side of my horse, and the charge passed harmlessly over. The man who fired attempted to mount his horse, which took fright and started off on a run with the man holding to the bridle and the horn of the saddle and making desperate efforts to mount. In a short distance I came up with him. He had given me such a close call that I was fully resolved to kill and ignore any offer of surrender.

Just as I was in the act of firing and only a few feet away, he let his horse go and called out, "I'll surrender." The words and the report of my pistol were almost simultaneous. He turned and fell full length on his face. I believed I had given him a death wound, but I fully intended shooting him again, but a cap caught in the cylinder of my pistol and it would not revolve.

I think he must have divined my intention, as he suddenly sprang to his feet and made a wild run down a steep rugged hill, falling two or three times over logs and brush. I easily kept near him, still trying to remove the cap but feeling sure of my man and still resolved to kill. Finally he fell over a fallen tree and seemed unable to rise.

Turning his face towards me, he begged me not to kill him. With that appeal for mercy, all desire to kill vanished. Rising partly up, he supplemented this appeal with the statement that his wife had recently died, leaving five helpless children depending on him for a home and support. On my assurance that he should suffer no further harm, he staggered to his feet and held out his hand, tears streaming down his face.

I took the offered hand and freely confess that sympathetic tears trickled down my cheeks. Such is the fickleness of the human heart: one moment ready to commit murder and the next melting with tenderness. His wound, though serious, proved not to be fatal, and I rejoiced later when I learned of his recovery.

I have never thought of this incident without feeling grateful for the part played by the cap in the cylinder of my pistol. This man's companion, who was with him behind the tree, threw down his gun and ran, jumping off of a bluff nearby, crossing a ravine and starting up a hill on the other side, was then shot down and killed by two of the boys as they sat on their horses on the edge of the bluff.

Returning to the main body, we found that they had surprised and captured a party of six of the previous night's raiders. These men had in their possession, when captured, a part of the booty taken on their raid, consisting mainly of bed clothing and wearing apparel.

There was an unwritten law among these independent commands that prisoners, when taken, were disposed of as their captors saw fit. That the captors of these men meant to kill all of them I had no doubt. Several miles away, on the return trip, a halt was made and the word passed around that the execution of the prisoners was soon to take place.

Among the prisoners was a man named Blackwell, of whom I knew something as to his general reputation, which had been considered good. I felt sure that this was the first time he had even engaged in jayhawking. He was a man of family and about 40 years of age. He was also a master Mason. There were only two Masons in the party besides myself, and the question with us was how could we save the life of this man? We discussed the matter among ourselves and resolved to make the effort.

A special guard had been selected by the Captain from among the most desperate men in the company, one for each prisoner. With my two associates, we rode up to the Captain just as they were ready to resume the march and said, "We will take this man." Our intention seemed to be understood, and they further understood that this action on our part was because this man was a Mason. A storm of protest was raised by men who declared Masonry should not save them and, for a time, the result seemed in doubt.

But we took our man and started back on the way we had come, leaving the others sitting on their horses. We had gone perhaps a half mile with our prisoner when a volley of small arms in the direction from which we had come told the fate of the other five men. Reaching a point in the woods where we felt our man would be safe, we bid him good-bye and told him he was at liberty to go. Returning along the road a short distance beyond where we had left the company, we saw, lying by the roadside, the five prisoners just as they had fallen when shot from their horses. I have always regretted that I did not make an effort to save the lives of these men. While to have done so would likely have resulted in the execution of six instead of five, but I would have felt better had I made the effort.

★ ★ ★

With the advent of Spring 1864, provisions for the people as well as forage for horses were well nigh exhausted. Luxuries such as sugar, coffee and tea were unknown even on the tables of the most fortunate. The plainest of food only was to be had and many families were already destitute and dependent on their more fortunate neighbors for bread.

The Federal troops stationed in the country drew their supplies from the homes of Confederates or Southern sympathizers. And as a result, the corn cribs and smoke houses of our friends were empty. Only by hiding as best they could the remnants of their supplies were they able to save anything in the way of provisions or feed.

Under these circumstances, to feed our horses or even accept food for ourselves made us feel that we were taking bread from the mouths of women and children. Yet we know that we were welcome to the best our friends were able to give us. The Southern women would, if it had been necessary, have crawled on their hands and knees, day or night, to supply our needs.

Our struggle to regain and hold control of the country against the odds that confronted us was utterly hopeless. Taking this view of the situation, a party of us, 12 in number, decided to make our way through the Federal lines on the Arkansas River and join the Confederate forces further south. The Federal forces, at this time in the country, consisted of one regiment, the Second Arkansas Cavalry commanded by Colonel John Phelps, and was stationed at Klepper Mill in the heart of the Crooked Creek Valley.

For some time past, the officers of this regiment had been threatening to banish Miss Baines or send her to prison, giving as a reason that she had on numerous occasions conveyed news to the Confederates and had in various ways been conspicuous for her disloyalty to the Union cause. Fearing they would put their threats into execution, we decided to marry, so that if it became necessary for her to leave home, I could make some arrangements for a home for her inside the Confederate lines. Many would doubtless think our conclusions under the circumstances very foolish as neither of us had any worldly possessions. But we had youth and health and a great store of love and hope, beside which the bauble wealth pales into insignificance.

Having made all necessary arrangements with my friends for our departure south on the morning of the 4th of April, and also having arranged with my sweetheart to meet me at the house of a friend on the morning of the third, we proceeded at once to the house of a Justice of the Peace under the Confederate States Government, accompanied by three friends. The Justice of the Peace was named Adair and his home was situated in a small field and about three miles from the Federal Camp.

Throwing the fence down near the house and also at the back of the field so we could pass out either way in the event Federals should appear on the scene, we dismounted and went into the house where the old squire, as briefly as possible, said the words that entitled me to say wife instead of sweetheart.

Remounting our horses, we rode back to the house from which we started, leaving the old squire and his family putting up the fence and destroying the tracks of our horses. Had the horse tracks about the house been found by the Federals, it would have meant the burning of his home. In less than an hour after our departure, a Federal scout was at the house.

The next morning only five of my friends showed up at the place of meeting; so after a short wait, we decided to wait another day for the other parties. In order to give our horses a day's needed rest, we decided to spend the day in an unfrequented piece of woods not far from my father's old home. Most of the houses had been burned in that neighborhood and, as very few people lived anywhere near, we thought there was less danger from scouting parties at that point. A public road lay about half a mile away and a creek between us and the road.

In the afternoon, a couple of us went to the creek to water our horses. While there, we saw a scout of 12 Federals with two wagons going toward the Federal camp, about three miles distant. Hurrying back to our friends, we decided we could not afford to let an opportunity like this pass.

Taking the road behind them, we overtook them about half way to their camps. I think we were in 30 steps of them before they discovered us. Four of them were riding behind the wagons, the rest in front. Riding behind two of the hindmost men were two women. At the first fire, these women let all hold go and tumbled to the ground. Of the four men riding behind, two were killed and two captured, one of whom was mortally wounded and died a day or so later.[*]

The other prisoner fell into my hands. Relieving him of his arms, I told him to care for his wounded comrade. He fully expected to be killed, and the reader can imagine how grateful he looked when told that he was at liberty to go. The Federals were so badly frightened that they never fired a shot. Being so near their camps, we knew they would hear the firing and would have scouts on our trail in a few minutes, so we separated, going in pairs, to meet again next morning. Before the set of sun, my companion and I were near and in sight of two scouting parties.

At daybreak the morning of the 5th, I bid my wife good-bye. Going to the meeting place agreed upon, my friends, 11 in number, were all present. Sorrowfully we turned our faces to the south, leaving our friends and loved ones to the mercy of an enemy, who had shown but little of that amiable quality in the past, and we had no reason to hope for improvement in the future.

Our trip across the Boston Mountains and through the Federal lines on the Arkansas River was uneventful for war times. We barely missed several scouting parties on the river and near by but came in contact with none. After a ride of five

---

[*]Union killed: Private Simeon Meek, Co. F, 2nd Arkansas Cavalry and possibly Private John Murray, Co. F, 2nd Arkansas Cavalry. The regimental history of the 2nd Arkansas Cavalry lists him as killed on Richland Creek, Arkansas.

days, we were inside the Confederate lines where we could lie down at night with a sense of security – a feeling to which we had been strangers for months.

After a few days rest, I reported to my command near Camden, Arkansas, two days after the battle of Jenkins Ferry.* My old regiment, the 16th Arkansas, had been consolidated with other Arkansas regiments. I was immediately put in charge of a detail of six men, with 30 or 40 head of horses belonging to dismounted men of the command, with orders to proceed to Southern Arkansas or Eastern Texas and sell for the benefit of the owners. This duty performed, I reported back to my regiment at Camden.

Under a reorganization of the command, I was assigned to duty as first lieutenant of the 4th Company, First Consolidated Regiment, Colonel Cravens in command. My captain was J.B. Cloud (Co. H, 16th Arkansas) of my old regiment. For some time we remained in the vicinity of Camden, later moving to Monticello some 50 miles east, where we spent the remainder of the summer.

★ ★ ★

The latter part of September, as well as I remember, while at Monticello, I received orders to proceed to North Arkansas for the purpose of recruiting for my company and regiment. This order was very gratifying to me, as I had grown somewhat weary of the monotony of camp life and longed for the more exciting life that I knew awaited me on the border.

General Price was then just starting on his famous raid in

---

*The Battle of Jenkins Ferry ended April 20, 1864.

Missouri. Joining Colonel Harrell's Battalion of General (W.L.) Cabell's Brigade, among whom I had many friends, I proceeded with them to a point north of the Arkansas River, near a village called Clinton in Van Buren County. I was honored with the command of the advance guard one day, but we encountered no Federals.

From near Clinton, with two men, we crossed the Boston Mountains, then infested and partially controlled by mountain Federals, who ranged over the country in small parties, drawing their supplies of arms and ammunition from the Federal posts on the Arkansas River. The second day's ride took us into a very rough mountainous country with narrow valleys and an occasional log cabin and small fields along the creek bottoms.

In one of these fields, we saw a man in Federal uniform gathering apples from a tree on the opposite side of the field and near a creek that ran just outside the fence. The fence being low, we jumped our horses over it, hoping to capture him in order to get information concerning any scouts that might be nearby.

As we entered the field he discovered us. Throwing his apples down, he jumped the fence and was across the creek by the time I reached the fence. I could see only his head and shoulders as he ran through some willow bushes, 40 or 50 yards away. Dismounting, I took deliberate aim, firing only one shot. I could see nothing further of him and told my companions I believed I had killed him. Throwing the fence down, they rode across the creek and found him lying on his face, dead with a bullet hole in the back of his head. I had no desire to see him and did not go over.

Quickening our gait, we rode three or four miles, passing several houses before stopping to make a statement of the occurrence. Riding up to a house near the road, a young woman, apparently 20 years of age answered our call. To her, we told the circumstances of the killing and described the place where the body could be found, little dreaming that she was the wife of the unfortunate man. The facts, as we learned later, were that her husband, with three or four other Federal infantrymen, were on their way home from one of the Federal points on the Arkansas River and had stopped nearby to rest, when this man went to get some apples with the result as stated above.

According to all rules of war, I was justified in what I did, but the facts as developed later made it a source of deep regret. Perhaps the thought of another young wife, who might be bereft in the same way, made me regret it more deeply than I other wise might have done.

The following day, we reached our home country in the Crooked Creek Valley. The Federal troops, who were stationed in the valley when I went away, left in the early part of the summer, but the country was still subject to the raiding parties from the north and south as formerly. There was still in the country a remnant of the Southern men who had remained during all the vicissitudes of the heartless, cruel struggle. Many had been killed in the unequal contest.

Old stone chimneys greeted us on every hand, silent monuments of once happy homes. Here and there a family living in some stable, crib or some old cabin not deemed worthy of the torch. The ones nearest and dearest to me I found in good health and cheerfully, hopefully, bearing their hardships and privations. The Federals, after I left in the spring, had treated my wife with some degree of kindness, due in part likely to the fact that I had set at liberty the two prisoners captured the day before my going away. I found my father's family living on the old home place, in an old log cabin that had long been used as a corn crib.

★ ★ ★

Partisan warfare was still being waged with more heartless cruelty than ever. The following incident will serve to illustrate something of the intense bitterness of the struggle for supremacy and revenge. Two brothers named Atchley lived near the boundary line between Carroll and Newton Counties. Each had a wife and a family of small children. Their sympathies were with the South, but they were taking no active part in the fierce struggle, preferring to keep out of harm's way and care for their families as best they could. They were noted as men of that quiet gentle disposition who would suffer wrong rather than have trouble.

They were surprised and captured at their homes by mountain Federals and brutally murdered in the presence of their wives and children. No appeal by their wives could touch the hearts of these men. These same men, sometime before this, had dragged a young man named Tyson from a sick bed, from which he was unable to move, out in the yard and killed him in the presence of his mother and other members of the family. The first of these incidents occurred only a few days before my arrival home.

The morning of the day on which I reached home, a party of Confederates, nine in number, all well known to me, started afoot into the section of country where these Federals lived. On their way, they passed by the homes of the Atchleys and heard from the lips of the bereaved widows the pitiful story of the murder of their husbands and looked into the mute, fear stricken faces of their innocent children. Can it be wondered that deep in their hearts was implanted a desire for revenge?

In this party of nine Confederates was the father and a brother, a boy in his teens, of the young man Tyson, who had been so brutally murdered as related above. Leaving the home of the Atchleys, this party made their way through the woods, evading all roads to prevent discovery, to the neighborhood of these mountain Federals.

Late in the evening of the second day out from a high point overlooking the valley below, they discovered a party of nine Federals killing and dressing a beef at a house in the valley. Keeping their presence concealed, they gradually drew nearer, keeping a close watch on every movement of the enemy. Observing that they turned their horses loose in a small field near the house, the Confederates rightly guessed that they meant to spend the night nearby.

In the early dusk of the evening, the Confederates drew nearer not losing sight of the enemy for a moment. Shortly after dark, they saw the Federals take their blankets and make their beds about 100 yards from the house in a peach orchard and near a fence on the bank of a creek. In the dim starlight, they were not able to tell whether all of the party went to the orchard or not, so they detailed two men to take positions near the house and await results. Waiting a short time for all to get quiet, the remaining seven crept single file along the outside of the fence, till opposite their unsuspecting foes. Here they waited for a short time and could plainly hear the conversation carried on by the Federals who were yet awake. They commented on the brightness of the stars and the great number of them.

Finally all grew quiet, when the Confederates noiselessly crossed the fence and at a distance of only a few yards, delivered such a well directed volley that only one of the party succeeded in getting to his feet, and he was promptly felled by a clubbed gun. Seven men lay in a heap, most of them just as they were lying when fired upon. To make sure, in the darkness that none should escape, pocket knives were brought into use and jugular veins severed. Doubtless the memory of a sick boy dragged from his bed to be murdered in the presence of his mother, whose prayers for mercy were unheeded and coupled with the pitiful story of the two widows the day previous, kindled in the hearts of these men that desire for vengeance that blood alone could appease. The two guards at the house, after the firing in the orchard, seeing no one attempting to escape hastened to the aid of their friends in the orchard, leaving the house unguarded from which two Federals later made their escape.

The next morning after their return, I saw these men with the horses, arms and bloody blankets of the slain who confirmed in every detail the story as related above. Incidentally, I will state that one of the men who participated in this affair which was called "the peach orchard scrap" was afterwards a member of Congress, for several terms from that congressional district.

★ ★ ★

The most frequent and persistent raiders of the Crooked Creek Valley came from the border counties of Missouri on the north. Led by Union men and deserters from the Confederate Army who had refugeed from Carroll and adjoining counties, who knew the country and the people, it was an easy matter for them from their places of comparative security to make raids through the valley, kill, rob, burn houses and drive off cattle and horses.

Shortly after my return home, a party of us, 15 strong, resolved on a retaliatory raid. The settlement we wished to strike was on the James River, about 75 miles distant. Starting one morning, we rode the first 50 miles by dark, through a section of country practically deserted. The night and the following day we spent on the White River, where we found a deserted field of corn, from which we fed our horses. Near nightfall we resumed our march, arriving near the Union settlement a little after midnight.

Tying our horses, we lay down in a cold drizzling rain for a short rest. With the break of day we were on the move. We knew a company of Federals too strong for us to cope with was stationed five miles distant on the river above us, so we struck the settlement near by hoping to find some of the men at their homes. In this we were only partially successful, finding two men only, one of whom was killed, the other escaping. We captured several head of horses. We expected pursuit as our trail could be easily followed on account of the soft condition of the ground, but none was made.

The most noted raider and house-burner from that section, and the most brutal, was Captain Jim (James M.)

Moore. The same party into whose hands I had fallen when wounded, his home was on Crane Creek between Cassville and Springfield, Missouri. In his house-burning and murderous raids through Carroll County, he claimed to be acting under orders from the general in command of the department, General (Edward R.) Canby[*], I believe. His statements were probably true, as we then understood such orders had been given. Regardless of his orders or what his duty as a soldier may have been, we felt a strong desire that he should be made to suffer for the wholesale burnings of our homes in the Crooked Creek Valley.

With this object in view and in the hope that we might surprise him or some of his men, we organized a scout of 15 men for the raid, camping the first night, some 20 miles on our way, at a farm house on Sugar Loaf Creek. Shortly after dark, we received word that a Federal Scout had gone into camp at the next house, about a mile distant. Their number estimated at 200. We concluded to give them a round or two. Leaving about half of our number with our horses, about half a mile distant from their camp, we proceeded on foot.

Coming to a small field of corn on the opposite side of which they were camped, we discovered that they had turned their horses loose in the field. We immediately conceived the idea of quietly making a capture of horses. Halting within a few steps of the fence for a moment's consultation, from this place we could see the horses. The moon being an hour or two high, some of the party suggested that we wait till the moon went down. Others more impulsive said, "Hell, no, we want those horses and we'll go and get 'em right now." With

---

[*]Major General, commanding the military Division of West Mississippi.

one accord we all started forward to be greeted by a volley of bullets from behind the fence, not over 30 feet away. We returned the fire and drove the guard away, but we got no horses, as the camp was now fully aroused.

The next morning we were joined by three brothers named Byrd, who, previous to the breaking out of the war, were neighbors of Captain Moore and knew him and the country well. With these men for guides, we proceeded on our way, reaching White River late in the evening. Here we found a deserted farm with a field of corn and a number of fat hogs running at large. Also an apple orchard laden with a bountiful crop of apples. Here we spent two days and nights, feeding and resting our horses and feasting on roast pork and apples, but without bread or salt.

Here we were joined by eight or nine others, making our force about 25 men. Late in the evening of the second day, we started on our ride of 40 miles or over, planning to reach the Moore home on Crane Creek at daybreak the next morning. With the exception of a brief stop to feed our horses about three o'clock in the morning, we were in the saddle all night.

Just at break of day we rode up to the Moore house. The wife and two daughters only were at home. We told them of the houses destroyed by Captain Moore in our country and the object of our visit. They entered no protest but said it was no more than they had been expecting. They were ladylike in their deportment and seemed to be above the average in intelligence.

Being in the enemy's country, we lost no time in applying the torch, and soon the buildings were a mass of flames. Looking back to the occurrence now, after a lapse of over 40 years, when all the bitterness engendered by the war is a thing of the past, I sincerely regret the burning of the Moore home; not through any sympathy or respect for him but because women were the immediate sufferers. But that was war, and "War is hell," said General (William T.) Sherman of the Federal Army, who made homeless more women and children than any other man in that great conflict.

It has always been a source of pleasure to me to contrast the orders of General (Robert E.) Lee in his invasion of Pennsylvania with the orders of General (Philip) Sheridan in Virginia and Sherman on his march through Georgia and the Carolinas. We could have burned many more homes had we chosen to do so, but we were content with the burning of the one, which was one of the objects of our long ride.

We surprised two men at their homes, one of who was killed, the other escaping. We learned after it was too late that the man killed was a non-combatant. His attempt to escape by running away from a house where we expected to find Federals led to his killing.

On our return trip, several miles away, we met a superior force of Federals and were forced to retreat, having one man killed in the skirmish that ensued. Whether the enemy suffered any loss, we never knew. We had expected pursuit as we learned that there was a considerable force of mounted men near where we had passed, so we kept a couple of men 100 yards or so in our rear to guard against surprise from that quarter and were somewhat surprised at meeting the force in our front. Dick Peel (Private Richard Peel, Co. E, 16th Arkansas) was the name of the young man killed. He was a fine young fellow and a good soldier. Some two hours after dark, we stopped for the night having been continuously in the saddle for over 30 hours, except the brief halt referred to the previous night and had traveled over 90 miles.

The time limit of my orders, 60 days, being nearly out, I got together what men I could, about 12 in number, and again bid goodbye to friends and loved ones, and set out on my return trip to my command. We passed through the Federal lines on the Arkansas River without incident worthy of note, crossing the river at Ozark. I reported to my command near Camden. Shortly afterwards we moved camp to Lewisville, about 50 miles distant, where we built log cabins and went into winter quarters.

★ ★ ★

About this time Captain Cloud was detailed for court martial duty, leaving me in command of the company, with Lieutenant Blackard, second in command.

Sometime in February 1865, we were ordered to camps near Minden, Louisiana. Many of the men were barefooted and otherwise ill prepared for a march in wintry weather. Those without shoes were given the option of remaining in camps until shoes could be had. But when marching orders were given, these men fell in line and tramped through the mud and cold without a word of complaint.

Our fare now and for several months past had been very poor. Corn meal of a very inferior grade, with a poorer quality of beef and sugar or molasses constituted our rations for practically all of the winter and spring of '65. Wheat flour was seldom to be had, and, when issued, we found it full of worms that made it almost unfit for use.

In the matter of pay, as well as my memory serves me now, we received two months pay in November and a like amount in March. Confederate money about this time was in specie about three to five cents on the dollar. But the matter of pay was a trifling factor with the Confederate soldier. The service rendered was as efficient and as cheerfully performed as would have been the case if payment had been made in gold.

The infantry forces of the Trans-Mississippi Department were in a high state efficiency at the time of General Lee's surrender. In looking over the official records of the war, I find reports of Federal spies, in which they comment at length of the discipline and efficiency of the Confederate troops.

A few weeks were spent in camps near Minden, when we were ordered to Shreveport and later to Marshall, Texas, where we received the news of Lee's surrender. I will not attempt to depict the gloom that pervaded our camps when the news was fully confirmed. General (Joseph E.) Johnston's surrender later convinced us of the utter hopelessness of further resistance. Many favored the disbandment of the regular army and the organization of independent commands and a resort to guerilla warfare. But wiser and more conservative counsel prevailed.

☆ ☆ ☆

After the surrender of Lee and Johnston, knowing that the end of the war was only a matter of a few days, a young friend, Captain Crump, and I resolved to secure mounts for a ride home, some 300 miles distant. With this end in view, we obtained leave of absence for a few days. We next arranged with a teamster of another brigade, for a consideration, to get a fellow teamster, and the two to saddle and mount two good mules and ride along a certain road, through a piece of thick woods after dark the following night, when Captain Crump and I were to meet them and play the part of highwaymen.

I was on time but Crump was late. A wait of a few minutes and I heard the teamsters coming. I must play the act alone or give it up. Stepping from behind a cluster of bushes, I seized the bridle of the mule ridden by the teamster who was ignorant of the plot and ordered them to dismount, emphasizing my demand with a slight punch in the side with the muzzle of my pistol. No further persuasion was needed as he hit the ground running, saying, "Don't shoot." The other fellow pretended resistance but soon left me in possession of two good government mules.

Mounting one and leading the other, I met Captain Crump a short distance away. I had some friends about 70 miles away in Southern Arkansas, where we arrived the second day following. Leaving our mules in the care of my friends for our future use, we set out afoot to rejoin our command.

A day's march from our camp, we met a part of my regiment, about 150 men, whose homes were in the northern part of Arkansas, on their way to Little Rock to surrender. They had their arms and camp equipage. As the surrender of the Trans-Mississippi forces had been agreed upon, it was now an option with men and officers as to the course they would take. I decided not to accompany the command to Little Rock.

Taking my orderly Sergeant George Burt (Co A, 16th Arkansas) and orderly Sergeant Newt Clark of the 5th

94

Company, splendid fellows and good soldiers, we returned to Marshall, hoping to secure mounts for them also. My friends and I fell in with General Shaver's Brigade on the march to Shreveport to surrender. On the way, we camped a few days at a village called Greenville.

Strolling through the woods one day, I found five bales of C.S. cotton hid in some thick woods. With the aid of a quartermaster who furnished transportation, we took possession of the cotton destroying all marks of ownership and sold it to a citizen for 50 Mexican silver dollars, which we divided equally. Cotton was then worth seventy cents a pound, but the belief was general that the Federal Government would confiscate all cotton regardless of ownership. This was the first money I came in possession of, after the close of the war, and 25 silver dollars was a big sum to me.

While camped at Greenville, on a fishing trip one day at a nearby lake, with Sergeant Burt, a friend named Wilson and one other whose name I have forgotten, we found on an island two C.S. Government mules tied in the thick woods. We quit fishing, took possession of the mules and swam them across an arm of the lake to the mainland. Here we were met by six men with rifles in their hands claiming ownership. We were also armed and by playing a bold game of bluff retained possession. We eased our conscience in the matter by reasoning that these men were at home, while there was a long weary stretch of over three hundred miles between us and our homes.

There being four of us and only two mules, it was now a question as to how we could make an equitable division. As I had some money I paid for one man's interest, 15 dollars I think. As neither one of the others had anything of value to give, they drew straws for possession, orderly Sergeant Burt being the winner.

On our return to camp, two of the boys took a near cut through a big plantation, and, in a piece of thickly wooded ground, discovered two tents, some covered wagons, camp equipage and about 20 head of fine horses and mules. Four or five men seemed to be the sole possessors.

We very easily came to the conclusion that these men had more than their share of Government property. So about ten o'clock, three of my friends, who were yet afoot, Clark, Wilson and one other, whose name I now forget, visited the camp and rode off three exceptionally fine mules.

All well mounted now, we rode towards home about 40 miles. Going to a farm house, we explained the situation, telling the owner all the facts in the case and requested him to keep our mules for us until we could go to Shreveport, get our paroles and return. This he cheerfully agreed to do.

We returned to Greenville and went with the command to Shreveport, arriving in the city just in time to witness the landing of the Federal troops under General Banks*, who came up Red River by transports. Quietly and without demonstration of any kind, the Federal troops relieved the Confederate guards, posted at various points and took possession of the city. The utmost good order prevailed. The surrender was a very informal affair. Small arms, artillery and other government property were deposited at various designated places. Several days were spent in making out paroles for the Confederates, before final disbandment.

---

*Major General, USA, Department of the Gulf.

Securing our paroles, my friends and I set out for home. We found our mules all right and were just weary enough after our 40 mile walk to enjoy a ride. Arriving at the home of my friends where Captain Crump and I had left our mules some days before, I was taken violently ill and was confined to my bed for several days. As I was among friends, my companions continued their journey home where they all arrived in due time.

My friend, Captain Crump, during this time had gotten his mule and started home going by the way of Clarksville, Arkansas, where was stationed a command of Federals, who appropriated his mule to their own use, so he had to walk the remainder of the distance; about 75 miles.

After recovery from my sickness, I started alone on my trip home. About a month previous to this time, while stationed at Shreveport, I had loaned a horse to a friend, Lieutenant McConnell (William H., Co. C, 16th Arkansas) of my regiment, who had obtained a leave of absence, with the view of getting his wife and baby from Clarksville, out of the Federal lines, to some place of safety inside the Confederate lines.

After a couple of days ride homeward, I met some friends who told me that Lieutenant McConnell and family had passed there a few days previous on his way to Clarksville, Texas. Being anxious to get my horse, I concluded to follow. A ride of three days took me to Clarksville to find that my horse had been stolen, while passing through southern Arkansas about a week previous.

Feeling somewhat disappointed, I turned my steps homeward again. After a ride of two days alone, I overtook three mounted ex-Confederate soldiers, two of whom I knew and who lived not far from my home. Meeting with these men was a great pleasure, as many miles of our route lay through a sparsely settled section of country noted for its outlawry. We found most of the people on our way in very destitute circumstances but ready to divide cheerfully anything they had in the way of provisions with a hungry Confederate soldier.

We arrived at the Arkansas River to find it nearly bank full and looking ugly to a landsman. There being no ferry, our only chance of crossing was by means of an ordinary skiff, which the owner proffered to loan us but would not undertake to row us over. I was the only one of the party who had ever used oars, and my experience was limited to a few short pulls in still water.

With some misgivings, we resolved to make the attempt. Taking the oars while the other parties looked after our horses, we pulled out. Two of the horses refused to swim, which made it harder for the oarsmen, but we effected a landing after a long hard pull nearly a mile below our place of starting. Not being accustomed to hard work during the War, I found before we were halfway across that blood was flowing freely from my hands.

We met several squads of Yankee soldiers after crossing the river but were not molested. We spent a day and night with my friends, Sergeant Clark and Lieutenant Blackard, who lived near Clarksville, and then resumed our journey across Boston Mountains to our homes in Carroll County, arriving there two days later.

My brothers were all at home, having preceded me some three or four weeks. I found my father's family living in the old log stable of which I have already mentioned, having been burned out since I was at home the previous fall.

While I have recited many incidents of barbarous cruelty, it should not be forgotten that there were many, many acts of kindness and heroic self-sacrifice, highly creditable to the soldiers of both armies. It has always been a source of gratification to me to recall that during that four years of bitter strife, I spoke no unkind word to an old man, a woman, a child or a prisoner.

This story was written as a result of numerous requests of grandchildren to tell them stories of the War Between the States. As I am a poor story teller, I promised to write for them something of my personal experiences, coupled with incidents that came under my observations. This I have endeavored to do, recording such events as I thought might be interesting to them. If it serves to impress upon their minds, even to a limited degree, the horrors of war and the blessings of peace, I will be amply repaid for my time and labor.

/s/ J.M. Bailey

J. M. Bailey is listed in Co. D, 16th Arkansas, as a Private/1st Lieutenant.

# BAILEY'S POST-WAR CAREER

Captain Bailey returned to the Crooked Creek Valley of Northwest Arkansas, near present day Harrison and Bellefonte, with his bride, Mary Matilda Baines Bailey. He found the countryside devastated from four years of war.

By using Federal Census records, I was able to trace the remaining years of his life.

Five years after the war, Bailey had overcome much adversity. He was a merchant and his personal estate was worth approximately $2,500. Bailey lived in Jefferson Township, Boone County. He had two sons; Ralph, age two, and Claude, six months old. A daughter, Daisy, joined the household on June 27, 1872. She lived 3-1/2 years before passing away on December 22, 1875. She was buried in the Bellefonte Cemetery.

Ten years later, Bailey was listed as a farmer. Twelve year old Ralph worked as a laborer. In April 1881, son Robert joined the family, but another son, John, born on February 10, 1886, died the next day. He was buried next to his sister.

Some time after John's death, the Baileys moved from Boone County, Arkansas to Texas. The 1900 Census records (the 1890 records for Arkansas were accidentally burned in a fire) show the Baileys living in Coleman County, Texas. Bailey farmed a homestead that he owned outright.

By 1910, the Baileys had moved to Nueces, Texas and lived in the Corpus Christi Ward 3. Ten years later, Bailey lived in Travis, Texas; in the Austin Ward. His sons had become quite successful. Ralph and Robert were doctors, while Claude had attended the Naval Academy and was serving in the Navy.

Mary passed away on February 16, 1927 in Austin, Texas. She was laid to rest in Bellefonte Cemetery next to her children.

After Mary's death, Bailey moved in with Ralph and his wife, Lucy, in Gatesville, Texas. He traveled to New York State to visit Claude, who, after retiring from the Navy as a lieutenant commander, owned a thriving apple orchard. During these trips, Bailey stopped in Boone County to visit his friends.

On June 5, 1930, Captain Bailey passed away at the age of 90. He rests next to Mary in his beloved Crooked Creek Valley.

I will always remember and memorialize Captain Bailey's reminisces of the war for his dash and daring as one of the "Last of the Cavaliers of the Old South."

James Troy Massey

# CAPTAIN J.M. BAILEY'S MILITARY RECORDS

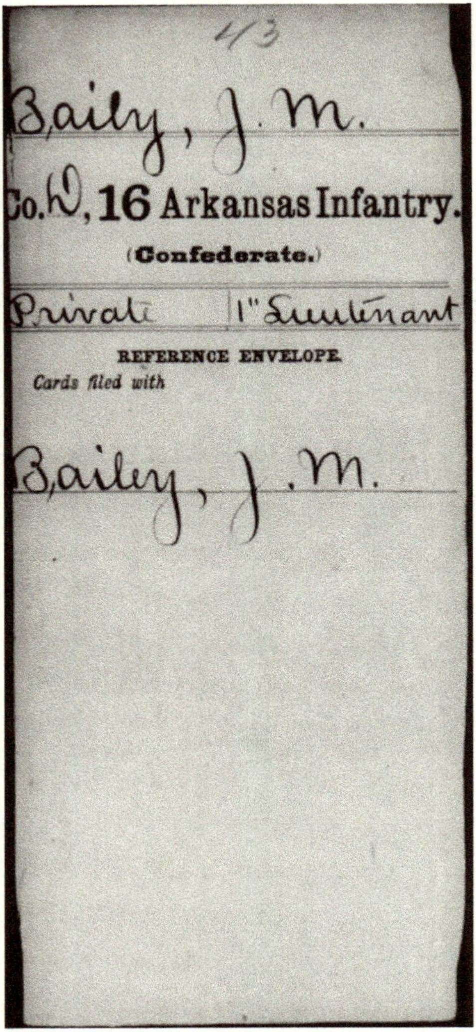

43

Baily, J. M.

Co. D, 16 Arkansas Infantry.

(Confederate.)

Private | 1st Lieutenant

REFERENCE ENVELOPE.

*Cards filed with*

Bailey, J. M.

Bailey, J.M.

Co. D, 16 Arkansas Infantry.

( Confederate. )

Private 1 Lieutenant

CARD NUMBERS.

| | | | |
|---|---|---|---|
| 1 | 4492908 92 | 20 | |
| 2 | 9960 | 21 | |
| 3 | 0017 | 22 | |
| 4 | 0084 | 23 | |
| 5 | 8664 | 24 | |
| 6 | | 25 | |
| 7 | | 26 | |
| 8 | | 27 | |
| 9 | | 28 | |
| 10 | | 29 | |
| 11 | | 30 | |
| 12 | | 31 | |
| 13 | | 32 | |
| 14 | | 33 | |
| 15 | | 34 | |
| 16 | | 35 | |
| 17 | | 36 | |
| 18 | | 37 | |
| 19 | | 38 | |

Number of medical cards herein _____

Number of personal papers herein _____

Book Mark: _____

See also _____

105

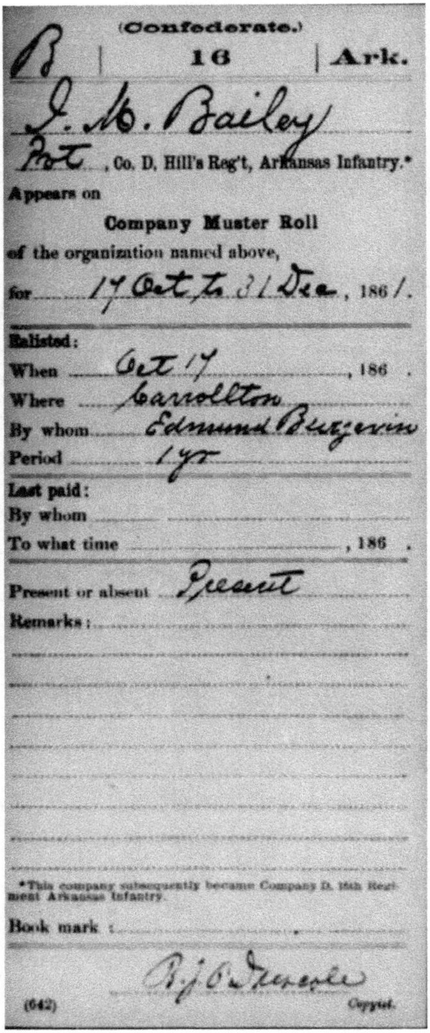

(Confederate.)

| B | 16 | Ark. |
|---|---|---|

J. M. Bailey

Pvt., Co. D, Hill's Reg't, Arkansas Infantry.*

Appears on

**Company Muster Roll**

of the organization named above,

for 17 Oct to 31 Dec, 1861.

Enlisted:

When Oct 17, 186 .

Where Carrollton

By whom Edmund Burgevin

Period 1 yr

Last paid:

By whom

To what time , 186 .

Present or absent Present

Remarks:

*This company subsequently became Company D, 16th Regiment Arkansas Infantry.

Book mark:

R. J. O'Donnell

(642) Copyist.

(Confederate.)

16    Ark.

J. M. Bailey

Pvt. , Co. D , 16 Reg't Arkansas Infantry.

Appears on

**Company Muster Roll**

of the organization named above.

for Jan r Feb , 1862.

Enlisted:
When Oct 17 , 186 1.
Where Carrolton. Ark.
By whom E. Burgevin
Period 1 year

Last paid:
By whom A. M. Ward
To what time 31 Oct , 186 1.

Present or absent Present
Remarks: Regimental Color Bearer
from Feb the 17 to the present.

Book mark:

(642)    B. J. O'Driscoll    Copyist

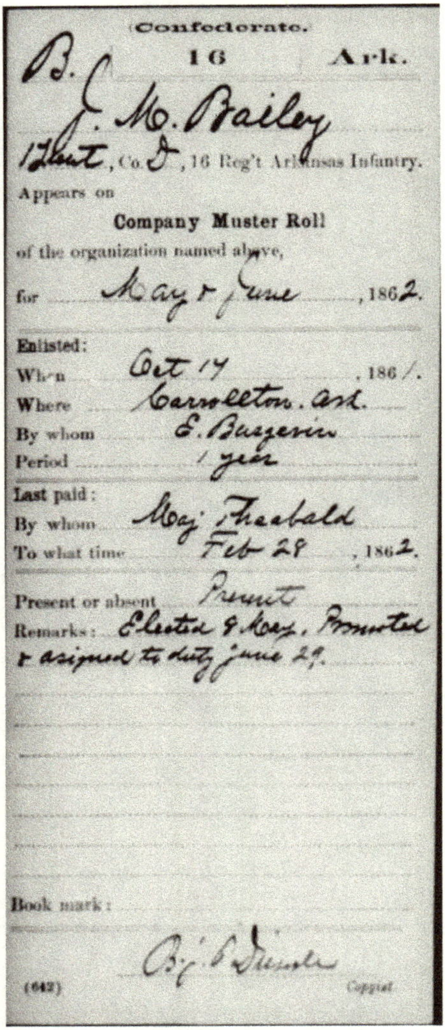

Confederate.

B. C 16 Ark.

J. M. Bailey

1 Lieut, Co. D, 16 Reg't Arkansas Infantry.

Appears on

**Company Muster Roll**

of the organization named above,

for May & June, 1862.

**Enlisted:**

When Oct 14, 1861.

Where Carrollton. Ark.

By whom E. Buzzerin

Period 1 year

**Last paid:**

By whom Maj. Theabald

To what time Feb 28, 1862.

Present or absent Present

Remarks: Elected 9 May. Promoted & assigned to duty June 29.

Book mark:

B. J. Dinole

(642) Copyist

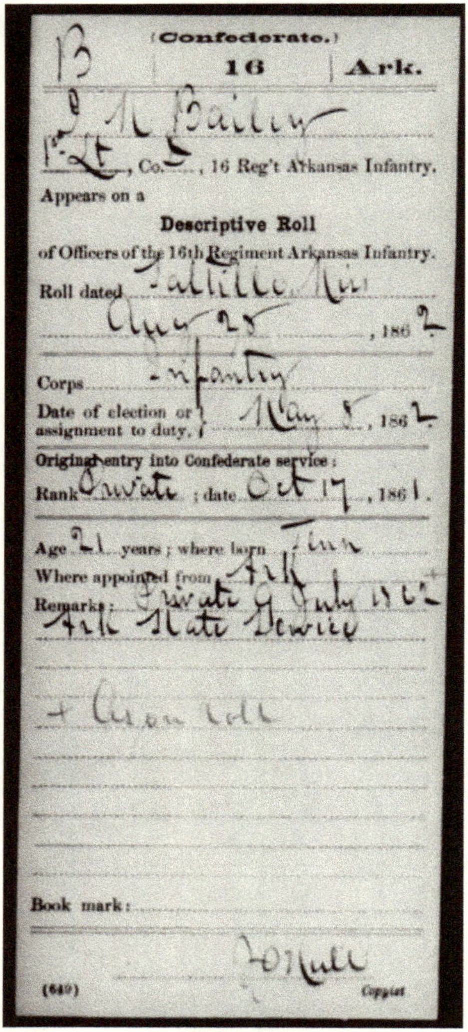

B (Confederate.) 16 Ark.

J. M. Bailey

1st Lt, Co. B, 16 Reg't Arkansas Infantry.

Appears on a

**Descriptive Roll**

of Officers of the 16th Regiment Arkansas Infantry.

Roll dated Saltillo Miss Apr 25, 1862

Corps Infantry

Date of election or assignment to duty, May 8, 1862

Original entry into Confederate service;

Rank Private; date Oct 17, 1861.

Age 21 years; where born Tenn

Where appointed from Ark

Remarks: Private G July 1862 Ark State Service

+ Also roll

Book mark:

(649) Copyist

```
            (CONFEDERATE)
    B    |  16                      Ark

    Joseph Bailey

    1st Lt  Co D, 16th Ark

Appears on a
                LIST
of commissioned officers present for
duty in the 1st, 3d and 4th Brigades
1st Division, Army of the West


List dated
                    Oct 13          , 186 2 .

Brigade            1st
Remarks
```

Box 42
No. 2
                    Shepherd
                        Copyist.

*Baily, J. M.*

1 Lt., Co. 4th Co, 1 Reg McNair's Brig.

**(Confederate.)**

/ **Inclosures.**

| | |
|---|---|
| Bed Cards | Final Statements |
| Burial Records | Furloughs or L. of A. |
| Certs. of Dis. for Discharge | Med. Certificates |
| C. M. Charges | Med. Des. Lists |
| Descriptive Lists | Orders |
| Discharge Certificates | Pris. of War Record / |
| Enlistment Papers | Resignations |

**Other papers relating to—**

| | |
|---|---|
| Admission to Hosp'l | Furlough or L. of A. |
| Casualty Sheet | Med. Examination |
| Confinement | Misc. Information |
| Contracts | Pay or Clothing |
| Death or Effects | Personal Reports |
| Desertion | Rank |
| Discharge from Hosp'l | Transfer to Hosp'l |
| Discharge from Service | Transportation |
| Duty | |

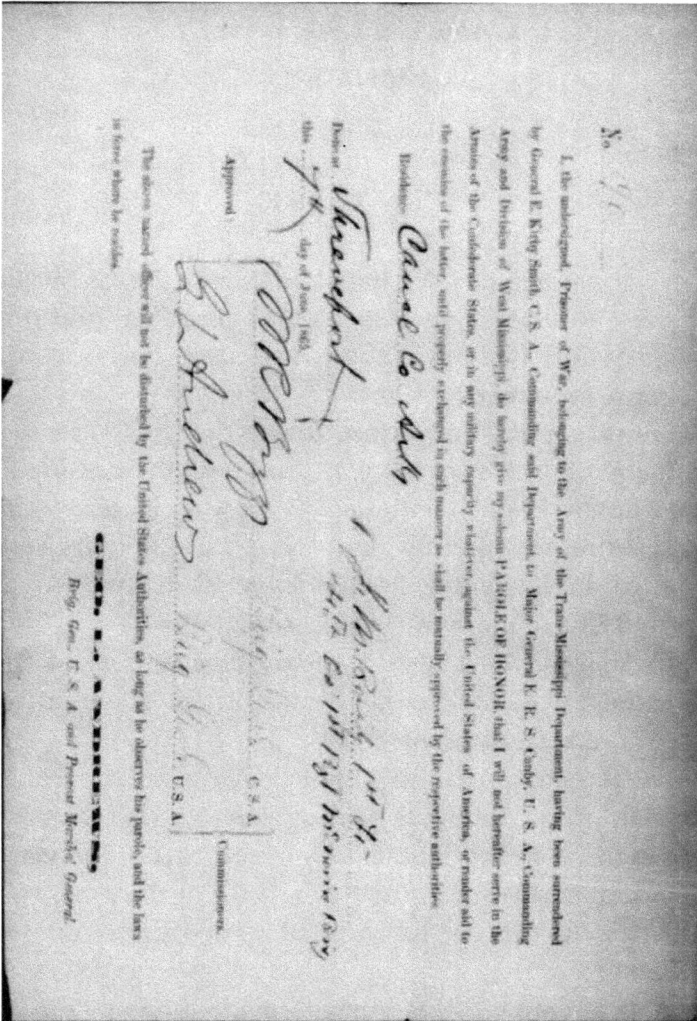

# CAPTAIN J.M. BAILEY
## OBITUARY

### From the *Harrison Daily*
### July 12, 1930

In the passing of J. M. Bailey of Austin, Texas on June 5, 1930, the *Times* loses one of its oldest subscribers and friends. Joe Bailey, or Captain Bailey, has been on our roll of subscribers for over 60 years.

He made a brilliant record during the Civil War, serving as captain at the close of the war. And with the passing of the years, Captain Bailey continued to grow in character and in mind. He dressed carefully, and the straight military carriage developed in his youth was notable as he moved about Harrison last summer with elastic step.

His bearing for a man of 89 was the marvel of friends here, who remarked that he would attract attention in the most cultured circles of the land.

The passing years did not leave Captain Bailey, a gentleman of the old South, out of step. He was widely read and living in New York State with a son part of the year and in his adopted state of Texas the balance of the time. He was in close touch with events and had a keen understanding of world affairs.

As an example of his interest in the home of his young manhood, he registered at Hotel Seville shortly after the opening and rejoiced as one of us in the progress of Harrison.

Before the Civil War, he lived on the farm, now the country estate of Mr. and Mrs. J.W. Bass. He came from a distinguished family, many members of whom were men of marked ability. The meager educational advances of the early days seemed to be no disadvantage to the Bailey family, as their own desire for knowledge was sufficient incentive to acquire an education.

Generations come and go, but we doubt if there will be any improvement on the type of citizen represented by Captain Bailey.

# MRS. MARY M. BAILEY
## OBITUARY

**From the *Harrison Times*
February 25, 1927**

Mrs. Mary M. Bailey, 85, wife of Captain J.M. Bailey, died at her home, 4109 Avenue F, Wednesday afternoon.

The body will be shipped by Charles B. Cook to San Antonio Thursday morning at 5 o'clock for cremation.

Captain and Mrs. Bailey had been married 63 years. Mrs. Bailey had been sick for several months.

Mrs. Bailey is survived by her husband and three sons, Dr. Ralph Bailey of Gatesville, Dr. Robert Bailey of Coleman and Lt. Commander Claude Bailey of the United States Navy. All of them were in Austin when their mother died.

**Mr. and Mrs. J.M. Bailey
With sons, Claude and Ralph and grandson, Clyde**

# Index

## A

Adair, Ben, 67
Adder, James, 75
*Albatross*, The, 31
Arkansas River, 24, 56, 79, 81, 83-84, 92, 98
Arkansas Troops
  14th Arkansas Infantry, 48
  16th Arkansas Infantry, 17-18, 20, 25-26, 32, 50, 65, 67, 74, 75, 82, 91, 94, 97
  17th Arkansas Infantry, 22
  1st Arkansas Calvary (US), 58
  1st Consolidated Regiment, 82
  27th Arkansas Infantry, 68
  2nd Arkansas Cavalry (US), 71, 79, 81
  3rd Arkansas Infantry (State Troops), 25
  4th Arkansas Company, 82
  5th Arkansas Company, 94
  Cabell's Brigade, 83
  Harrell's Cavalry Battalion, 10, 67, 82
  Reid's Arkansas Battery, 14
  River's Battery, 25
  Shaver's Brigade, 94
Army of the Trans-Mississippi (CSA), 94
*Auld Lang Syne*, 12

## B

Bailey, Adelia, 2

Bailey, Caloway Shields, 4
Bailey, John, 1-2
Bailey, John Meriman, 3-4
Bailey, Lewis, 2
Bailey, Lewis Washington, 4, 67-68
Bailey, Malinda Jane, 3, 9-10
Bailey, Mary Matilda, 71, 73, 79
Bailey, Milita, 2
Bailey, Nancy, 2
Bailey, William, 1
Bailey, William Wilson, 3-4, 12, 18, 22, 25, 54
Banks, Nathaniel P., 31, 38, 41, 96
Baton Rouge, (LA), 31
Bellefonte, (AR), 9, 69
Beller, Irvin, 67
Benton, (TN), 2
Berry, James H., 29, 48, 49
Berry, William D., 49, 65, 66
Blackard, Hezekiah, 48, 92, 98
Bloody Hill, Battle of, 16
Bolivar, (TN), 29
Boone, Dan, 48
Boston Mountains, 19, 24, 81, 83, 98
Brittain, John, 25
Buchannan, Mark, 25, 29, 42
Burt, George, 94-95

## C

Cabell, W.L., 83

Camden, (AR), 82, 92
Camp Walker, 12-13
Canby, Edward R., 89
Cane Hill College, 11
Cassville, (MO), 88
Cecil, John, 56, 65, 74
Clark, Newt, 94, 96, 98
Clarksville, (AR), 24, 97, 98
Clarksville, (TX), 97
Clinton, (AR), 83
Cloud, J.B., 37, 82, 92
Cockrell, F.M., 28
Corinth, (MS), 24-27, 32, 49, 52
Corn, Nancy, 2
Crane Creek, 88, 90
Cravens, Jesse L., 48, 82
Crooked Creek, 9, 69
Crooked Creek Valley, 5, 65, 67-
69, 74, 79, 84, 87, 89
Cross Hollows, (AR), 19
Crump, George, 48, 93-94, 96-97
Cunningham, Bershaba, 3
Cunningham, Joseph, 3
Curtis, Samuel, 19

**D**

De Valls Bluff, (AR), 24
Deering, Guinn, 67

**E**

Easter, William, 8
Elkhorn Tavern, 23
Elm Springs, (AR), 18
Enterprise, (MS), 26

**F**

Farmington, (MS), 25
Fayetteville, (AR), 18
Fort Smith, (AR), 56

**G**

Gardner, Franklin, 38, 40-41
Grant, Ulysses S., 26
Greenlee, Jeff, 12
Greenville, (LA), 94-96

**H**

Harrison Cemetery, 10
Harrison, (AR), 5, 10
*Hartford*, The, 31
Hatchie River, 29-30
Herbert, Louis, 20
Hill, J.F., 18, 21
Hiwassee Purchase, 2
Hiwassee River, 2-3
Holly Springs, (MS), 30
Holmes, Mose, 51
Hopper, Towne, 53, 54

**I**

Iuka, (MS), 26

**J**

Jackson, (MS), 30
James River, 88
Jenkins Ferry, Battle of, 82
Joe Wright Guard, 12
Joe Wright Guards, 12, 14, 18
Johnson, Jones, 12
Johnson's Island, 43

118

Johnston, Joseph E., 93

**K**

Kelly, Henry C., 71
Klepper Mill, (AR), 69, 79

**L**

Lawson, William R., 48
Lee, Robert E., 91, 93
Lewisville, (AR), 92
Lincoln, Abraham, 11
Little Rock, (AR), 49, 56, 94
Little, Lewis, 26
Lyon, Nathaniel, 13, 16

**M**

Maine Troops
  25th Maine Infantry, 39
Marshall, (TX), 93-94
Marshall's Prairie, (AR), 68-69
McConnell, William H,, 48, 97
McCulloch, Benjamin, 13, 19-23
McIntosh, James, 20
McKennon, Arch S., 39-40
Meadows, David C., 48
Meek, Simeon, 81
Memphis, (TN), 24
Minden, (LA), 92-93
Mississippi River, 24, 30, 48-49
*Mississippi*, The, 31
Missouri Troops
  1st Missouri Brigade, 26, 28, 30
Mitchell, E.G., 25, 30, 50
Monticello, (AR), 82
Moore, James, 50
Moore, James M., 88, 90

Murray, John, 81

**N**

New York Troops
  165th Zouaves, 33

**O**

Ocoee River, 1, 3
Okolona, (MS), 26-27
Owens, Joe, 12
Ozark, (AR), 49, 92

**P**

Parker, James, 67
Parker, Thomas, 42
Pea Ridge, (AR), 19
Pea Ridge, Battle of, 25
Peel, Richard, 91
Phelps, John, 79
Pike, Albert, 23
Pittman, J.M., 25, 39
Pittsburg Landing, (MS), 24
Pixlee, B.T., 22, 25, 29, 37
Port Hudson, (LA), 30-31, 41, 47-49, 65
Poyner, William S., 43, 46, 49
Price, Sterling, 13, 19, 20, 82
Province, David, 25

**R**

Rector, F.A., 22
Red River, 96
Richland Creek, (AR), 81
Rienzi, (MS), 24
Robertson, Lewis, 17
Rosson, John, 10

www.ingramcontent.com/pod-product-compliance
Lightning Source LLC
LaVergne TN
LVHW091153080426
835509LV00006B/671